Love
Found
and
Lost

Love Found and Lost

The Kim Vui Story

Kim Vui

TEXAS TECH UNIVERSITY PRESS

This book is typeset in EB Garamond. The paper used in this book meets the minimum requirements of ANSI/NISO Z39.48-1992 (R1997). ∞

Designed by Hannah Gaskamp
Cover design by Hannah Gaskamp

Library of Congress Cataloging-in-Publication Data
Names: Kim Vui, 1939– author. Title: Love Found and Lost / Kim Vui.
Description: Lubbock: Texas Tech University Press, 2022. | Includes index. |
Summary: "Memoir of Kim Vui, dancer, singer, and 1960s and 1970s film actress of South Vietnam, the 'Sophia Loren of Saigon'"—Provided by publisher.
Identifiers: LCCN 2021005712 (print) | LCCN 2021005713 (ebook) |
ISBN 978-1-68283-091-8 (paperback) | ISBN 978-1-68283-092-5 (ebook)
Subjects: LCSH: Kim Vui, 1939– | Motion picture actors and actresses—Vietnam (Republic)—Biography. | Women entertainers—Vietnam (Republic)—Biography.
Classification: LCC PN2889.89.K564 A3 2021 (print) | LCC PN2889.89.K564 (ebook) |
DDC 791.4302/8092 [B]—dc23
LC record available at https://lccn.loc.gov/2021005712
LC ebook record available at https://lccn.loc.gov/2021005713

Printed in the United States of America
22 23 24 25 26 27 28 29 30 / 9 8 7 6 5 4 3 2 1

Texas Tech University Press
Box 41037
Lubbock, Texas 79409-1037 USA
800.832.4042
ttup@ttu.edu
www.ttupress.org

For my mother, born in Tra Vinh, buried in Virginia

Contents

Illustrations

Introduction

I was born during war. That was in 1939, when Japan was already fighting in China, and shortly before German aggression in Europe would have historians set that year as the beginning of the Second World War. While I was still a young girl, some Vietnamese fought to resist the return of French colonial control, while others supported puppet governments serving foreign rule. With scarcely a pause, I matured as a young woman, mother, singer, and actress, during the period of American civil and military operations in Viet Nam.

War shaped all the circumstances of decision-making for my parents when I was a child. Just a few years later the same was true for me. Moving family from Saigon to a presumed comparatively safe Dalat in 1963, followed by a loveless marriage and then departure from Viet Nam almost ten years later, always fearing for the safety of my own children, is reflective of issues and experiences that tormented millions of Vietnamese people. All that happened during those years shaped my life, even including today, as I revive memories and place them before you.

It is thought by many observers that entertainers are so self-centered and superficial that they must be insensitive to significant events and the sociopolitical tensions around them. This is not true for me. In fact, I believe that fame derived from accomplishment in the arts, sports, or any field of endeavor devolves a special responsibility upon we who are recognized for the excellence of our performance. We should be especially observant, considerate, and at times even comforting of others. Fame adds weight to our every choice of social and even political expression. We can be a positive element within society, and consequently we need to take care.

As a popular singer, then actress and sometimes painter, I found performing and creating was always within my Vietnamese national context. I did sing some foreign songs, but most of my music and film roles were not disconnected from the lives of other Vietnamese. Moreover, the popularity derived from my appearance and personality provided an opportunity for me to be informed about contemporary events and to assess ambitions relative to abilities. I was not just an empty-headed pretty face.

A deep regret, looking back, is that although a perceptive observer, I did not participate in political development. I was more concerned for my family's welfare than anything else, and that is typical for most Vietnamese women because of the expectations placed upon us by our parents. I do not know whether that cultural characteristic will change in the new Viet Nam, or for Vietnamese living in America, but it was certainly authentic and pervasive for my generation.

Memories from Viet Nam are still bound tightly within me even though I now live in the United States of America. I love the country of my birth and worry for Viet Nam. I love equally the country of my new citizenship and care for America's future. I also understand that for everyone born in Viet Nam and now becoming an American citizen, the transition may be awkward, perhaps even painful. It is tempting to carry old attitudes forward rather than adapt to a new and different environment. Some may think themselves part of an outpost in America from which change can be radiated back to the homeland. We need to ask ourselves whether looking backward is constructive or alternately evasive. Are old attitudes foundational for our children born in a new land? Are we retroactively thinking, or will we be new Americans? We who were Vietnamese and became Vietnamese American can help newcomers make the transition. If there are some among us, not ideal-motivated, who prey upon the confused or linguistically challenged, we must identify and avoid them.

I know everyone in my new country refers to the "Vietnam War" when describing events of 1955–1975, while in Viet Nam that traumatic period is now called the "American War." I think of those years as encompassing both civil and military operations in Viet Nam and weighty decisions made in Washington. Political action was as important, as calculated and miscalculated, as combat operations; and in fact, the military dimension emerged from an initial civil and political lack of success. Problems between Vietnamese and Americans, and a mutual frustration, were in some part a consequence of national differences.

Be assured, I am not providing another history or account of even one aspect of a particular war; however, a few notes throughout the text may provide a useful sketch of individuals or events mentioned within my personal story. In this context, I want to express my appreciation for consistent encouragement from Tam Minh Kapuscinska, PhD, daughter of Tran Ngoc Chau (who parted from this world in June 2020). I will always remember and be grateful for assistance and support provided by Jerry and Thao Dodson. Travis Snyder and Christie Perlmutter, editors for TTU Press, kept me moving forward and suggested improvements for both accuracy and readability. Jen Weers provided the professional indexing that was beyond my own ability to arrange.

People assume the life of an actress, or any beautiful woman, is an entirely smooth road from one high point of easy living to another. I say instead that life for any woman will always be a challenge. My own is one within which I have been more often sad than happy, and so until now I have always kept my deepest feelings private.

My two special and enduring loves were for my country of birth and for a certain man. Few people knew that the love of my life chose a path diverging from mine. There were brief opportunities to reconcile, but then, and later while still in Viet Nam, we did not reconnect. War sometimes may bring people together, and subsequently the same war can separate them.

I also lost my country. Of course, I don't mean lost as in the sense of carelessly misplacing car keys, or that Viet Nam in any way disappeared. You can find it on a map. One can travel there. The Vietnamese people survive and endure, as they have in one form or another for two thousand years. But the Viet Nam of my childhood, of my life as a young woman, is no more.

It is from those feelings of loss, from my very personal perspective, that I speak to you now of love found and lost.

Others have written exaggeratedly about me, occasionally to demean, sometimes to flatter; but what follows is my story, in my own words, spoken from my heart, at times with pain, and now shared with friends who will read this book.

KIM VUI

CALIFORNIA – VIRGINIA 2021

Love
Found
and
Lost

CHAPTER 1
Escape to Tra Vinh

I was little more than six years old when my family fled chaos in and around Saigon. It was September 1945. French soldiers and police, released from detention, were beginning to reimpose colonial rule in Viet Nam after being set aside by Japan during World War II. Soldiers from Japan had maintained order in the streets, sometimes ruthlessly, after taking complete control from the French earlier that spring; but later in August Japan surrendered to America, and the next month Ho Chi Minh declared Viet Nam independent.

Vietnamese nationalists armed themselves with whatever weapons they could buy or steal and then sought to take control of Saigon while frequently beating or even killing any French wherever they could be found. Cruel acts were justified, many claimed, because those foreigners were representatives of colonial repression. If not, why were they in our country? The Binh Xuyen (a well-known racketeering gang) chose to demonstrate patriotic sentiment by killing foreign and mixed-blood women and children.

British forces arrived, supposedly to disarm the Japanese, but instead ordered Japanese military to restore security by driving nationalists from Saigon. Previously, those same Japanese soldiers were strict but usually correct in behavior. Now Japanese brutality was unrestrained. Just a few houses from where our family lived, a young man was seized by them because he was suspected of having taken wire from fencing around a police post. Everyone in the neighborhood was ordered to assemble and witness the consequences. Father had to bring me because otherwise I would be home alone, not advisable in those days. The young man, barely more than a boy, was forcibly shaved of hair, ear to ear, and then topped with tar before being tied to a chair placed in the sun. His screams and sobs while radiant solar energy cooked his brain were silenced only when his head was chopped off. We knew that, according to our folk belief, he was doomed to wander forever as *con ma*, a ghost.

French residents, previously detained by Vietnamese nationalists, were now released and rearmed by the British. Regaining control in Saigon, the revived French avenged themselves upon Vietnamese. Anyone could be murdered, anytime, anywhere, all for the cause of restoring order. Not one part of the city was more secure than any other.

Families ran away to rural areas for safety. My father had relatives in the Go Vap area of Gia Dinh Province, but that would have been no refuge. The suburban hamlet was so close to Saigon that there was as much chance for violence there as in downtown city streets. So, my parents decided to make their way, with their daughter, to Mother's home province, Tra Vinh. We left with other families from the Cho Lon waterfront, all of us on, what seemed to me, an enormous rice barge. Our vessel was one of many moving away from the city. The direction was generally west, toward branches of the great Mekong River, along a trail of canals that in better times brought rice to Saigon for shipment northward within our own country and outward to international markets.

I remember that the canal water was deeply colored from earth eroding along the edges. When shaded by occasional clouds, we floated on a band of dark chocolate brown. But by sunset and with the reflection off the canal surface, we seemed amidst liquid gold. Soft wavelets off our bow were like billows from rolls of fabric tossed in the air and unfurling over market counters. Insects with iridescent wings flew low over the water, sometimes even among the barge passengers. Lightning bugs danced among us just after sunset. I was the only child on board, so I amused myself by capturing a few snails and setting them to slow race on the deck planking. I was oblivious to the danger.

As we drifted through Long An Province, toward My Tho and Ben Tre, this part of our country seemed quiet compared with Saigon. We rode high in the water because, although crowded, the barge was burdened with much less weight than when filled with rice. So long ago was our travel that now I do not remember what powered our train of barges. We proceeded most languidly, barely moving. I recall that sometimes men attached rope to a barge and walked along the canal bank to move us forward. The land around, so quiet, seemed almost abandoned. Occasionally, made possible by our slow movement, those few on shore would call out in greeting and later make farewells by wishing us a safe journey. We travelers simply waved in reply, while drifting away and onward. Our first night's sleep was on that same barge. Being excited but tired, I do not remember more, no matter how hard I try . . . except that Mother and Father were tense, seeming fearful, despite floating further and further from conflicted Saigon.

Late on the second day we transferred to a smaller, and dirty, old boat, so crammed with other families that the stuttering engine could barely propel the nervous passengers across a broad branch of the Mekong River from My Tho to the Ben Tre landing. We arrived there at nightfall, on a muddy shore by a small clearing made dark and forbidding by the density of the surrounding coconut grove. The following morning, we would all transfer to even smaller boats that could weave through much narrower waterways toward another Mekong branch separating Ben Tre and Tra Vinh

Provinces. I was too excited, even though very tired, to sleep easily. Placed between Mother and Father, I could listen to their nervous whispers. I understand now, remembering much that followed, that they feared the unforeseen, the unpredictability, inherent in each stage of our flight south.

My parents did not know that the Mekong Delta provinces were also suffused with violence, not of the street-fighting anti-colonial Saigon city form but no less vicious. Five years earlier, in late 1940, there had been rural revolts in the south, especially severe in scale and duration in My Tho and Ben Tre, the very two provinces we were transiting on our way to Tra Vinh. French military and police, not yet subservient to Japanese command, suppressed the revolts. Their instruments for restoring colonial order, believed legitimate for the purpose of maintaining control over we Vietnamese, included bombing and the massacre of demonstrators. Simmering hatred for the French and any Vietnamese affiliated with them lingered. Now in late 1945 everyone traveling in this region, especially if suspected of sympathy for the restoration of foreign rule, moved at risk to their lives.

The moment small boats poled ashore to a coconut grove, my family (even I) could feel a change of mood among all the travelers, a shift from nervous confidence to diminishing hope and even burgeoning fear. The men who would crew those boats to move us further southward stared malignantly at the Saigon travelers. They spoke roughly while moving around us, even rudely bumping into the passengers while demanding fees for transport to further destinations. The Saigon families who began the shared travel on large rice barges were gradually divided out as smaller packages to separate destinations. We would be on a boat carrying one other family toward Tra Vinh. Our lives were in the hands of the boat chief and three of his men who worked oars and poles.

We were soon snarled in life-or-death trouble when, just before midday, the crew chief asked Father why he was so nicely dressed in a country of poor patriots. He had noticed Father's relatively fine Saigon tailored shirt; when grabbed from behind by one of the oarsmen, a faux-French label was discerned. That was enough to prompt another of the boatmen to sarcastically ask whether aping French dress meant support for French rule. Making matters worse, my father, although entirely Vietnamese by birth, had an atypical facial appearance that could be taken for mixed European.

Suddenly, all three of the crew, claiming themselves patriots, accused Father of being *viet gian* a (traitor) and began to pummel him back and forth between themselves. While still yelling accusatory curses they bound his hands behind his back, attached a large stone to a length of rope, and tied the other end around his neck. Despite his fearful denials and pleading, the crew pushed him to one side of the boat and were obviously prepared to throw him overboard into muddy waters. He surely would have been drowned, had mother not fallen to her knees, pulling me down beside her, and even while begging for his life, produced jewelry from the folds of her clothing as trade.

The leader frowned, calculated, and finally told one of the others to pull Father back from the railing. Not for the last time, my mother had to be protector for the family. Those pirates, as I later thought of them, may not have been as anti-colonial and patriotic as they claimed. It could have been just an instance of theft, and perhaps even spur-of-the-moment lust for my mother, with disposal of Father as superfluous. Had they succeeded, I might also have been thrown overboard as simply one more inconvenience.

Reprieved, my father huddled with his daughter, little me, while Mother spoke sweetly, soothingly, and convincingly to those boatmen about Vietnamese love for country, why this was the most important time for Vietnamese to pull together, to help all Vietnamese, to defend Viet Nam and obtain independence. My mother was young and pretty, and her words softly spoken in southern dialect, sounding beautiful to the ear, conveyed that persuasive message. In better times the boatmen might not have menaced us, but the unpredictability of those days seemed to allow license for anyone with a loose conscience.

The remainder of that day was passed by our moving through a labyrinth of narrow waterways before crossing the small channel that bisects Ben Tre Province. Finally, we arrived at the second of two main branches of the Mekong River. We slept on the bank within another coconut grove. The crew that had threatened, then attacked, Father, but after Mother's intercession delivered us to this resting place, now cautioned my parents that travel onward to and around Tra Vinh would be the most dangerous part of our journey. We did not believe them, thinking that they so spoke just to mitigate their own rough behavior.

But when night cloaked weary travelers, Mother drew Father and me together, close to herself, and spoke quietly of bad feeling across the river between Khmer Krom (Cambodians) and Vietnamese. My father was as ignorant as myself on all geography beyond Saigon. Mother explained that long ago, most of what we Vietnamese considered *nam phan* (the southern part of our own country) had been part of Cambodia, and even earlier it was ruled by a magic kingdom called Phu Nam. When Vietnamese people moved southward and seized land from those who had preceded them, the Khmer Krom resented rule by the newly arrived Vietnamese who placed themselves above all others. I would surely have forgotten the history shared with us, except that for many years afterward my mother would occasionally remind me of the year when we escaped Saigon. I never failed to remember those days in peril, our lives threatened, and even danger within the anticipated sanctuary of Tra Vinh. I learned that when the world turns upside down, family can only depend on family, and family should always be ready to protect family.

The next morning, while passing a small mid-channel island before approaching Tra Vinh town, we saw several bodies bobbing in the water. Some had been tied together in an awkward bundle embrace. I stared until mother covered my eyes and held me close. Soon our boat nudged ashore. One by one, with Mother leading, we climbed up slippery bamboo and timber lattice laid over the river-bank and landed at the province capital town.

Although Mother had sent a desperate letter to her family, we learned later that it never arrived. Now in Tra Vinh no one waited to meet us, to take us in hand. All around was noisy confusion. The people here seemed antagonistic, even with each other. Mother quietly told us to move as though sewn tightly together, because streets in this town might be divided against each other according to whether Khmer Krom, Chinese, or Vietnamese (Buddhist or Catholic) dominated. We had no relatives, no friends, not even slight acquaintances to advise us. That first night we sheltered in a shabby, foul-smelling, open-sided market with nothing to eat. The next day, really without alternative, my parents decided to press onward to Rach Loc hamlet, mother's childhood home, where we could shelter from the murderous environment surrounding us. My grandfather, grandmother, other relatives, and their friends would protect us. But first we had to reach them!

In all the years after, right up to these days when I set my personal story on the pages before you, I have never forgotten what I witnessed on the road from town to distant hamlet. Not far from the market where we had fitfully slept, along the single-lane dirt track that we walked with others, there were bodies strewn on both sides, even some far into adjoining fields and paddies. These were not the remains of people who had simply died and were not yet buried, nor even bodies of unfortunates killed in fighting between groups of rival affiliation. We were seeing the tragic residue of human beings who had been murdered, hacked to death. Most of them were partially stripped of clothing, either to humiliate or because garments were valued more highly than the lives of the people who had worn them.

At midday we were stopped by a carousing band of drunk, rough, and cruel-appearing men, all in black rural garb of simple shirt and trousers, each bearing a club, long knife, or spear. They fired accusatory questions in Vietnamese at us while speaking Cambodian among themselves. They wanted, it seemed most of all, to know whether we were local or *o ngoai* (outside)—that is, from somewhere beyond Tra Vinh. Father, lacking a regional accent, was hopeless in this situation, so Mother responded for all three of us, most fortunately speaking with her childhood lower Mekong Delta inflection. She explained that we were from Tra Vinh but had been trapped by the war in Saigon and were now fleeing French soldiers and Vietnamese thieves to return home.

We had some bread, purchased that morning in the shabby Tra Vinh town market, and Mother handed over some chunks of elongated loaves for the men to share. Their acceptance was a positive sign matching my mother's gesture. Moreover, she could speak a few Cambodian words. Her way of responding to this crisis, as on the small boat with the pirates, was once again a foundation for our family's survival.

But we still had to pass a test, crude, cruel, and inhumane, for onward passage. The marauding gang insisted that we each had to eat a portion of flesh from one of their fresh kills. In truth, I did not comprehend at first what was demanded of us. Mother saved me by pleading that I, a mere child and sick, could be excused, while she and Father would prove themselves as asked. My parents did as necessary, although I still cannot, even now, understand how they were able to do what had to be done. We were allowed onward passage.

As we were walking slowly away, very carefully so as to not stir an instinct for pursuit, I looked back and saw those same men pressing around another group of travelers while screaming "*Kap Youn! Kap Youn!*" (chop—to kill—Vietnamese), even while we three who were Vietnamese were allowed escape thanks to Mother. Over the passage of many years, she more than once reminded me that the very human gesture of offering provisions, even something as simple as bread, may diminish the cruel intent of another person. People are hesitant, she would always say, to kill another person with whom they have just shared food.

Before our travel southward, my parents were told by some friends that the central and northern Viet Nam provinces were suffering famine. The cause was American bombing of the north–south rail line and coastal shipping supporting the Japanese military. But those same trains and small ships were an essential part of the Vietnamese economy. So, although southern rice production was barely affected, the provinces north of Saigon that were always partially dependent on rice shipments from Mekong Delta provinces were now dramatically food deficient. The railroad was soon inoperable, and during the last months of war coastal shipping was nonexistent. The situation was made worse by increased requisitioning imposed by Japan to provide for their army, police, and those Vietnamese who cooperated with them.

But we were traveling in the south, not in any way a food deficit area. There was no explanation for cannibalism except that it had to have been a revival of a symbolic ritual, some residual primitive folk belief, ignited by ethnic Cambodian rage for revenge upon Vietnamese.

After two long painful days, feet swollen and bleeding, sometimes pulling rice seedlings from paddies to gnaw on, we wearily arrived at my mother's birthplace hamlet, where her own mother and father still lived. We were warmly, and loudly, welcomed. I never complained along the way, during that long walk, but I was exhausted, weary of muscle and bone-heavy. Now, within my mother's family embrace, I felt soothed, enveloped by love from the people who would care for us.

Our arrival at Mother's old home and reconnection with her kin was right at the end of the harvest cycle for the spring–summer rice fields. Grandfather explained that all the hamlets in Tra Vinh

Province grew rice for two crops each year, and this meant working the paddy fields almost constantly. There was a continuous rotational cycle, beginning with intensively working the soil as preparation for receiving transplanted seedlings, placing them, and then watching over their growth until ready for harvest. The color of the fields changed with each phase, like different shades of jade: brown when bare; later green, beginning with a pale tone and then deeper in hue; and a slight golden tint at harvest. There was no end to the work for every family member, except when fields were briefly fallow; but in return there would always be abundant food, surplus for sale to rice merchants, and even some remainder to home brew *ba xi de* (rice wine) for relieving the aches and pains of almost constant labor.

Homes nestled in the shade of great trees with extensive limbs, all so thick of foliage that each tree resembled a giant umbrella. Banana trees, with leaves broad enough to cut and fashion into fans, grew close to each house. Along the small streams traversing the hamlet, and at the edge of paddy fields, were graceful coconut palms. Each home was screened from others by trees and plants growing around it, yet there was a sense of overall hamlet togetherness. The houses were all made of wood, with an open courtyard of packed earth before each one. Entry into the home was directly from that yard to a family reception room with an altar usually facing arriving visitors. Our grandparents' altar supported numerous family photographs and small Catholic religious figures. Traditional Buddhist symbols were carved deeply into dark wood, reflective of rural folk belief of centuries past. Sleeping areas were to the side of the reception area that was also space for family activity. Food preparation and cooking areas were always placed to the rear. Supporting columns and beams for the roof and walls were of dense insect-impermeable wood. Rafters provided convenient storage space. Most homes had thatched roofs, with only a few boasting clay tiles. Mother told us that her family could afford tile, but it was best—prudent—to avoid any display of comparative wealth that might tickle envy.

Ducks and chickens, lots of them, moved freely throughout the hamlet, around homes, and in and out of the rice fields. There were a few elegant but mean-tempered geese here and there. Just once having been chased and nipped by one of those feathered aristocrats would persuade you to avoid teasing them. I was therefore more fascinated by the cute ducklings and their frenetic reaction to my chasing them. Despite my best efforts, it was not possible to catch one. Then my grandmother explained that when pursued a duck would always escape by besting a little girl's reaction time. However, if I sat quietly, a few would come closer and I could feed them until little by little, one might accept a gentle touch. A life lesson that applies to more than ducklings, and for Grandmother immediately beneficial by causing me, at least temporarily, to be less hyperactive than usual.

My only complaint, expressed to my grandfather, was that girls were not allowed to tend water buffalo. Regarded by everyone as "lords of the fields" and virtually members of the family, each buffalo was precious, and by tradition only boys were assigned responsibility for their care. I thought that most unfair, but Grandfather explained the real reason was to keep boys so busy that they would not have time for teasing pretty girls. I was not much mollified. Once I persuaded a cousin to let me ride his family buffalo while he played with friends. I was scolded for flouting a countryside custom, scolded even more severely than my cousin had been for relinquishing his charge.

We children were everywhere, around and underfoot, overhead hiding in the rafters, and a constant bother to parents and other adults. Even when at our worst, though, we were usually tolerated with good humor. In fact, just by being the next generation, guaranteeing hamlet immortality, we were kindly indulged for representing the future. Each child had a nickname, often funny, and children were called and even referred to by that name rather than by the rarely used proper birth registration one. In this way envious, malevolent, or at the very least mischievous spirits could not easily identify, then injure or steal health or life from, a little boy or girl.

13

I loved all my cousins, and there were many, but my favorite was a recently married young woman. She was beautiful, with hair that fell to her waist when unbound for combing. She was already pregnant, with a swollen tummy. I was allowed to place my hand gently upon her stomach and feel movement within. Nothing conveys more appreciation for the miracle of life than lightly touching through thin skin and flesh the movement of an infant soon to be born.

All around the hamlet, and in streams and small pools within, there was water, because even in the dry season the previous accumulation lingered. Just before the rainy season, water buffaloes would seek out moist spots and make them muddy by rolling around to seek relief from insect bites. When the dark monsoon clouds began to drench the land, all the previously dry streams and shallow mud wallows would flood. Rice seedling beds could be carefully tended while paddy fields were irrigated to prepare for transplanted rice shoots. As streams and ponds expanded to fill their margins, ducks brought forth ducklings. We children, like those ducklings, would play in and around the water. In the evening, parents and grandparents, with visiting neighbors, sipped from small teacups that might contain rice wine. They would socialize by gossiping or telling stories, recounting what had been told many times before. Children would listen until, eyes heavy from day-long play, we would find our way to the soft places provided for sleep. I knew that we who had fled here for refuge were loved and in a safe place.

Years later, Mother explained that Grandfather was a member of the hamlet management committee. Ordinarily a hamlet committee acted in a social role, sometimes even mediated conflicts occurring within the hamlet; but now my grandfather and a few others persuaded families that the safety of the community required sounding an alarm when strangers approached. So everyone, relatively poor or well off, Buddhist or Catholic, participated. Of course, at the time we children were simply told to keep our eyes open for the unusual, to be alert even while playing, and to tell the nearest adult if anything seemed different from the ordinary. The next step would be to raise the loudest possible noise to get the attention of everyone working in our fields. Bamboo staves were struck rapidly against each other, staccato-like, making a sharp slapping noise. Anything metal, even cooking pots and pans, must be banged against other metal to generate a clanging and ringing sound.

Our crude system was almost immediately tested when Cambodian thieves armed with spears and knives attacked. Alerted, almost everyone scattered into adjacent woods. The few raiders who dared follow in pursuit were surrounded, set upon, and beaten by our own men. So, word spread that incursion into our village area of several hamlets would be less easy than elsewhere. Even so, the youngest son of a wealthy family, although cautioned, once rode a pony too far on an oxcart trail. His body, head almost severed, was found the next day in a drainage ditch, covered with leaches and so hacked that it was as though one cut had been struck for each of his short sixteen years of life.

But slowly, that kind of communal violence—which we had witnessed during travel, experienced again when our hamlet was raided, and saw emphasized by the murder of the young pony rider—gradually subsided. Connection between the hamlets, travel to the village center and market that served our cluster of hamlets, and even a trip to Tra Vinh town, were safe again. No one really knew what brought about the more tolerant behavior. People might have just tired of a life suffused by anger and fear, and the meanest villains who had emerged to murder others may have either been killed in turn or shrank away in shame. Who could tell?

Father was less than content with this new countryside life. There was really nothing for him to do. In truth, there was nothing useful that he could do. He tried fishing, but as a non-swimmer Father was nervous even when alongside a narrow stream or shallow pond. So, he was more threat to himself than to the fish. Once Mother had to save Father by pulling him from a nearby canal after he tripped and fell while trying to separate fish from a carefully placed net. He was so anxious, fearful of death by drowning, that when desperately grasping my mother he almost dragged her beneath the water.

Tra Vinh Province, by rural economy, custom, and even speech pattern, was completely foreign for my father. Although grateful for the refuge provided by mother's country family, he missed his familiar and beloved Saigon. Father would often catch a ride by oxcart to the next community. Referred to as a village, it was a sort of local inter-hamlet center and market. Roads were either rutted and dusty by the fall–winter dry season or else slippery with deep mud during the spring–summer monsoon rain. No one would casually travel out from the hamlet, but Father had an almost desperate need for tea and conversation with the few others who, like himself, had fled from Saigon and were incapable of adjusting to country life. So unintentionally, by default, he became our tenuous link to news from other parts of Viet Nam.

One day, more than a year after our arrival in Tra Vinh, Father returned from one of his market diversions and relayed some important news. Some equally discontented and gossiping tea-drinking friends had received letters from Saigon reporting that the city was overflowing, as never before, with French soldiers. Colonial police totally controlled Saigon, and a French army was beginning to spread outward to the provinces. Father speculated that we would soon see them nearby, even in my grandfather's small Tra Vinh hamlet. We hoped not.

A few days later, two strangers carrying the same news visited. But their perspective was entirely different. My grandfather seemed prescient in telling neighbors and family members that those two would visit each family, one by one, to speak about the changes in every part of Viet Nam. He thought they would probably describe resistance to French colonial reoccupation and then perhaps suggest what every Vietnamese should do. Grandfather advised each family, even including the children, to listen civilly because everyone needed to understand what was happening in our country and how our families might be affected.

Those two men who eventually crossed the courtyard and asked permission to enter our home were dressed as commonly as any hamlet farmer, but after sitting and courteously sipping tea, they spoke more firmly and insistently than we were accustomed to hearing. They announced that they represented the Viet Nam Giai Phong Quan (Viet Nam Liberation Army), and this army included every Vietnamese of any age, religion, or level of education, all the millions of people who loved our Mekong countryside, everyone who loved the whole country from Ca Mau in the south to Hai Phong of the north. This army of Vietnamese people was coming together to resist the French restoration of dirty colonial rule. Our struggle, they told us, might require more than a year, more than five years or even ten years, but with everybody working for country, over time resistance led by the Liberation Army would certainly win independence for Viet Nam.

"What should you, Tra Vinh families, do right here in your hamlet?" They rhetorically asked, and then answered their own query, continuing in a determined voice:

> When French soldiers come, and they will . . . do not bow in fear. Do not provide information, labor, or guides . . . even for money. Do only the minimum inescapable if in fear for your life or necessary for family survival. Lie if you must respond to questions. Misdirect them. Hide your young men and women. General resistance everywhere means that the French will have to stretch very thinly across our entire country, and so they will not be able to maintain themselves everywhere with only a few traitorous puppets in a few hamlets. They will raid here and there and withdraw from here and there. They may return, but with declining effectiveness each time. For every action there will be stronger reaction. Hatred for the French will be inflamed province by

province until finally a great fire sweeps across the land. The French will be so burned that they can do nothing other than withdraw.

The older of those two passionately speaking men concluded by confiding that very soon other Liberation Army representatives would visit to explain how we should contribute to the national resistance movement for connecting every hamlet and province. They declined another small cup of tea; after all, stopping at every house, how many token cups could they consume? They departed my grandparents' home and walked toward the next. The following day they left our small community to travel to another.

Our family members—and, we soon learned, other hamlet residents too—had mixed reactions. Some young men were already deciding to meet with the next visitors expected to come help organize resistance. I think, having played with them, that each boy, even the youngest, wanted to be a hero. They dreamed of becoming real soldiers for Viet Nam. Grandfather was persuaded, and explained to others in the family, with children eavesdropping, that the time for cooperation with, or even grudging acquiescence to, French-appointed governors and their agents, had passed, gone forever. He was hopeful that Buddhists and Catholics, and even our Cambodian neighbors, would put aside mutual aggravation and rivalry for the benefit of our country. Grandmother was hesitant, indicating as a principal interest preserving the family, and while thinking of the nation, avoiding risk to life, especially that of the children.

Mother and Father were silent, probably believing that since they were not permanent residents, opinions should most appropriately be expressed by those who had always, and would always, be of the hamlet. And I, not yet eight years old, was simply living in the moment, very observant but oblivious of implications beyond tomorrow.

Then one day, early in 1947, the French came knocking. It was just at the beginning of the rainy season, so roads from Tra Vinh town to districts and hamlets were more easily traveled than they would be a month or so later. Still, we had practiced our crude alarms, and we expected some warning. There was none. Suddenly, there they were, soldiers advancing across almost dry paddy fields toward our thatched houses clustered under sheltering trees. Some people ran to hide in thickets along the streams, many more grouped together by family in courtyards before their homes, and a few simply knelt and prayed for some deity to interpose between themselves and men with obvious violent intent. There was no opposition. The people in my grandparents' hamlet had not yet the time needed, nor the promised guidance, to organize resistance.

Mother reacted more quickly than most, leading me to the rear of a home and placing me among storage jars and baskets to hide while she went to find my father. I was not afraid, but I was definitely confused because of the noise, people screaming and sounds of something like firecrackers, only somehow knowing that was not what I heard. Vietnamese, my people, did not have guns in our homes, so it could only be the French soldiers advancing across rice fields while shooting rifles. I crouched as small as possible, like a little ball of compressed flesh and bone, and prayed that Mother would come back to me that second, or the next, or the next. There was turmoil all around, people running past my hiding place, incomprehensible screams. I felt at the center of explosive commotion but simultaneously awfully alone.

Then I heard a different kind of cry, a baby crying, that suddenly stopped. A woman screamed and I remembered that my shamble of baskets and jars hiding place was just behind my beautiful cousin's house, the young woman who when pregnant had allowed my palming her swollen tummy. I pressed closely to the side of the house and peered through cracks in the wall. Then I became a fearful witness to terrifying violence. So young was I, then at seven years of innocence, that the nature of the witnessed crime was not immediately understood. A pale-faced French soldier, and another but black with scars on his face, were holding my cousin down on the floor, spreading her legs wide for a third invader to force himself upon her. Still another was standing back, laughing. When my cousin screamed again the two holding her on the floor hit her, striking hard, until she stopped.

Just then my mother came from behind, gripped me by my upper arm, and with Father in tow dragged me away ever more deeply toward the rear of our hamlet. There, where neatly tended foliage became wild growth, where broken baskets and fractured ceramics accumulated, they thrust me into a large, cracked water storage jar lying on its side and threw old moldy bananas and leaves over all of it. Mother squeezed my lips so tightly together that they hurt, while telling me to be quiet, not to make a sound, if I wanted to live even just one more day. She took Father by the hand and pulled him away in a different direction, probably hoping that separation would make survival of at least one more likely than not. I made no sound, but for hours could not stop my lonely shaking. My silent tears flowed without cessation.

The French, white and black (Senegalese, or from some other African colony, Father later guessed), marched away late that same day. They stole small pigs, chickens, and ducks—at least those they could catch—and shot, seemingly for fun, as many others as they could. They tried to take our water buffaloes, but the family beasts were not easily led, so many of them were simply shot for sport or incidental meanness. Some houses were burned, and some were spared. The pattern, or rather lack of pattern, was entirely whim and nothing else. Several people were beaten, and a few young men taken away with the departing invaders. My cousin was not the only woman raped that day, but she was the only one who, following the next sunrise, died. Her husband had been one of those right at the beginning, caught in the fields, bound and marched away to an uncertain, and never known, fate. All who remained, especially her mother and father, mourned my cousin and the baby who had preceded her to a miserable death. My eighth birthday was a few days later, but no one could celebrate while so many survivors of violence were wretched.

Liberation Army people, but not the two men who visited a few months before, arrived a few days after the French soldiers rampaged among us leaving homes and other nearby hamlets devastated. These new arrivals carried weapons and a had tough, confident air about them. They suggested that organizing should not be simply for alarm but also for community defense that would be a necessary part of the national resistance. Everyone—that is, among the adults, because children were of course only listening—eventually agreed that the time had come to support a national army for independence. Some young men, from those who had been absent or evaded capture during the French raid, volunteered to follow our visitors away for training. I remember that everyone appeared excited. Only a few showed apprehensions that we were right at the edge of an unknown life-altering change. Most committed unhesitatingly to the goal of national independence.

My mother and father made a family-centered decision. After lengthy private conversation together, they decided that despite witnessing French crimes against Vietnamese, despite accepting the principle of resistance, our family should return to Saigon. When we fled from the city, their choice was because of disorder and murder on Saigon streets. Now, no matter to what extent the hated French resumed authority, Saigon would be safer than the war beginning in every province.

Mother also instructed me, insisting by squeezing my arm, that I should constantly, without even one day's exception, wear a crucifix around my neck. She believed it was visible life insurance, because French and African colonial soldiers would be less likely to rape and kill a Catholic girl while there were so many others who were not. And for several years she would check my neck each day, each evening, to make sure that the protective talisman was with me.

CHAPTER 2

Return to Saigon

y mother, Nguyen Thi Ky, went to Saigon before the Second World War for work and, if opportunity allowed, to study. Her rural family was reluctant to approve travel so far from the Tra Vinh home. But her Mekong Delta extended family held sufficient land to provide surplus rice every year for sale to middlemen rice brokers contracting for milling and delivery to the great market area of Cho Lon adjacent to Saigon. So, the family rationalized that my mother, although young, might usefully keep family and friends informed of Saigon conditions and prices.

My father, Dang Phu Tho, was a peripheral member of a Saigon petty merchant family. By fate or simple accident, my parents met and by social natural selection were soon common-law husband and wife. A few years later, I was born on May 12, 1939, in Cho Lon, registered and baptized Nguyen Thi Vui. My parents had a child three years previously, but she died too young. Thus, in some sense, I was their second chance. My physiognomy at birth caused a stir among the neighbors because three equally spaced dark post-natal circles appeared on my scalp, not yet covered by hair and thus clearly visible. Some neighbors, suffused with traditional folk belief, swore that I had been obviously blessed by Buddha and would be especially protected all my life. Mother, fervent Catholic, feared church scandal and so every day would soap and vigorously scrub my scalp. Eventually, the controversy faded as the marks themselves disappeared.

The neighborhood to which we returned from Tra Vinh was across the Ben Nghe Canal from Cho Lon. The canal was originally a natural stream draining to the Saigon River before it was cleared, made deeper and wider, and commercialized. Now it very distinctly separated the largely Chinese-populated and crowded Cho Lon market streets from our comparatively semi-rural area. Coming here, for me, was not so different in its immediate surroundings from life in Tra Vinh. I was still playing with chickens, ducks and ant armies and indulged by relatives and neighbors. Having learned, like other country children, to use a sling shot, I often took mine to a nearby cemetery and scarred commemorative tablets by making them my targets. I was content to be alone, but if playing with neighborhood children I expected to be the leader and would always make sure all others would follow me.

And play, for me at eight years of age, was more important than school. I had not attended any classes in Tra Vinh, so it was not easy to catch up to these Saigon boys and girls who were already performing at a certain grade level. I thought of school as a diversion from neighborhood games. Classes in dance, drawing, and introduction to watercolor were enjoyable, and I loved writing our beautiful Vietnamese language, careful to make every correct mark for phonetics and tone. The school was administered by the Catholic Church, and with an intentional linkage to the foreign power that had introduced Catholicism, the French language was prominent in the classroom. Pride induced me to work hard, and soon I caught up to most of the other students.

I was a neighborhood favorite by the time I was ten. Whenever possible I helped nearby elderly women, many alone by day while younger family members were out to work as laborers on the Cho

Lon and Saigon docks. I carried water for those lonely ladies, ran errands, and would childishly sing and dance to please them. Those older women were my first audience, and I was in turn theirs while they told me stories and Vietnamese fairy tales and entertained themselves with local gossip while I listened. They were my out-of-classroom educators.

I was still innocent—that is to say, entirely naive—concerning the strength and multidimensional nature of sexual attraction between men and women. Once, some years earlier during the Japanese occupation and while American planes were bombing Saigon, I was crowded with many others in a rudimentary earthen bomb shelter near the cemetery. A man—I thought of him as an old man—had sat behind me and clasped my back tightly to his own body. Being then a simple child of only six years, I thought it was for my protection, but I felt something hard poking the fabric of my trousers, and that seemed wrong. Afterward I always took care to avoid him. Remembering that early unpleasantness, and having seen rape in a Tra Vinh hamlet, I equated sexual behavior with assault and brutality. My menstruation began sooner than was typical and frightened me. Mother and aunts had yet to speak of that which is biologic and inevitable. They explained that my first blood was earlier than usual, and they had thought it too soon to speak of "the birds and the bees."

At twelve and thirteen years old it seemed to me that boys, even men, regarded me differently. Crude expressions of regard for my appearance annoyed me and made me wary. When I carried water for elderly neighbors, typically in two metal containers, each suspended from opposite ends of a long pole, nearby boys stared. The need to balance pole and prevent spillage required a swaying, somewhat rhythmic, stride and movement of body. And my body was developing the sort of curves that fascinate men. Older boys began to follow me home from school. I was often bothered by their jostling me enough to spill my school bag and thereby have an excuse to come closer while helping to pick up books and pencils. It was always worse when it rained, because the thin fabric of the typical school uniform, a white *ao dai* (Vietnamese long tight tunic worn over white or black pantaloons), would stick to my body. When I complained to my father, rather than comfort me he would suggest that I must have been encouraging or teasing boys and young men. Mother was much more sympathetic and understanding but had no satisfactory solution for me. "Just be very careful," she warned. Eventually, the intrusive boy problem was so irritating and troublesome that a cousin, a policeman, determined to wait for me after school. He would accompany me, glaring at the young men, until we were in sight of my home.

My initiation, excitation, and actual ignition for becoming an entertainer was in church. Mother was sure that salvation in this life, as well as a guarantee for the promised everlasting one, would be assured by the closest possible connection to the Catholic faith. She required me to attend Mass, make confession, and take communion. I could easily do all that, although being questioned in the confessional about my feelings for boys seemed intrusive. But what I adored about church was the opportunity to raise my voice in hymn. Several members of the church lived in our semi-rural quarter, and having heard me singing for fun, unschooled but with a strong, clear voice, proposed me for consideration as member of the youth choir.

To this very day, while reflecting on the past—disappointments, misunderstandings, and my own mistakes, remembering history witnessed in my country at war, everything grinding within me for metamorphosis to the woman I am today—I acknowledge that my personal behavior is influenced by a societal mélange of Catholicism and Vietnamese folk Buddhism. The two are not antithetical in purpose. Indeed, they are complementary, perhaps for Vietnamese even supplementary, one to the other. Some degree of syncretic spiritual belief seems to be a part of being Vietnamese, and I do not have in mind the Cao Dai faith with a cosmology including Joan of Arc, Louis Pasteur, and Vladimir Lenin. Vietnamese Buddhists and

Catholics in general have a lingering respect for spirits of the field, special rocks and trees, and the whispering passage of the departed, ghosts and the unexplainable. Each lunar New Year (Tet), Buddhists and Catholics gather at local temples to consult fortune-tellers adept in prediction for the immediate future.

Notwithstanding the broad folk belief acknowledged and accepted within Vietnamese society, I will always be grateful for my first Catholic Church choir introducing me to the power of voice lifted in song. Our *cong doan* (congregation) was larger than those of many other churches, so we had a large youth choir. Our young choral group was frequently invited to visit and sing for other congregations, especially in nearby rural areas around Thu Duc and Bien Hoa.

Even there, not far from Saigon, clashes were frequent between Viet Minh and local security units paid and directed by the French. During one of our trips beyond the city, we were frightened when a gang attacked the church where we sang. Whatever their intent may have been, whatever reasoning, if any, those men waving machetes and short swords hacked at some of the local Catholics who just moments before had welcomed us. I crawled into shrubs behind the church, not entirely concealed because my backside protruded, but perhaps the attackers thought me already dead and so I was left unharmed. Were those bandits communist-organized and -directed Viet Minh, or were we exposed to violence as a consequence of some local dispute? We could not know.

On another occasion when I was not yet fourteen, we traveled to a small church near Tan Uyen, not far from Bien Hoa town. Before we could properly organize ourselves for song, before much of an audience was assembled, several men entered the church with guns and called out their intent to kill traitors. A priest pushed me in the direction of a large closet wherein robes were hung; other children were pushed in behind me. I hid myself beneath as many folds of fabric as possible, shaking, while hearing shots fired. When sounds of gunfire were replaced by wails and cries of grief, I crawled out. The priest, some local parishioners, and even young boys and girls from my Saigon church were bleeding, a few dead or dying. After we returned home our church decided the youth chorus should not continue to travel to congregations in countryside districts and provinces.

Witnessing tragedy, even being a small part of one, could not turn me from music. When not with the church choir, and really only wanting to amuse myself but also sparked by making neighbors happy and enlivening afternoons while my parents were at work, I would sing and dance along our street while staying carefully close to home. Surprisingly, I was invited to sing for a wedding party at one of the neighbors' houses, and then at another, where one of the guests, a restaurant owner, asked me to entertain twice a week in the evening. Although I was excited, Mother and Father were apprehensive. I was still very young—they thought too young—but believing that I had some talent, they finally approved . . . with limits. A family member would always have to accompany me, and I should continue school. So, singing and dancing, but still innocent and only unconsciously sensual, publicized by word of mouth and always escorted by a relative, I was more and more in demand as an attraction for modest local restaurants, neighborhood clubs, and parties.

Small theaters in Saigon and Cho Lon neighborhoods hosted variety shows that were called "opera," meaning that thematic short dramas would be played on stage, and between those acts singers and dancers would take turns performing while scenery was altered behind curtain. There was a similarity to what was called "vaudeville" in America of an earlier period. Hoang Cao Tan, owner of Saigon's biggest radio station, and his associate Minh Trang, who was also a singer, managed the most popular troupe. After seeing me entertain neighbors, they took me on as a sort of protégée and introduced me during company performances as a new young and rising entertainer. They provided me with my first contract and,

I adopted a unique appearance as a teenaged dancer and singer.

thinking that my birth name lacked "sparkle," made a slight alteration from simple Vui (happiness) to Kim Vui (golden happiness). And so I was best known by that name through all the years that followed, even until now.

I knew that more money would be earned in theater venues than restaurants, but my voice had not yet acquired the range and strength that I achieved later. So, while still a "mid-teenager" I also danced, at first a variation on ballet, but later transitioned to a sort of cabaret exotic dance. I would return home so tired after an engagement that sleep would only arrive when an aunt massaged my aching limbs. Even though I was earning money for Mother and Father and was a successful member of a theatrical troupe, I was not satisfied. Kim Vui wanted to be a singer rather than a dancer, and I was fairly stubborn about pursuing that goal. So, Hoang Cao Tan and Minh Trang introduced me to Le Do, who was a gifted teacher and guitarist with an unfortunate affection for the opium pipe.

After hearing me sing and gauging my range, he made a new Vietnamese arrangement of the "Blue Danube" waltz for me. Another Vietnamese singer, Thai Thanh, had already sung that waltz so beautifully that it was the standard against which I would be judged. Le Do coached me to something better than just acceptable competence. The first time that I sang "Blue Danube" in the theater, people stood, yelled, and clapped loudly, forever it seemed, and I was afraid that so much noise indicated disapproval. But I was wrong. Instead, this was a first hint, a step towards the beginning of fame. Children, some older and some even younger than me, began to enthusiastically greet Mother and me in the local markets. Sometimes so many clustered around that I was a little frightened. I asked Mother why they would follow us up and down aisles from stall to stall, and she replied that it was for their sweet love of me.

The most significant socioeconomic/political/police/criminal organization in the Cho Lon and Khanh Hoi area of greater Saigon during that period was the Binh Xuyen group. It will seem strange to a non-Vietnamese reader that an organization was simultaneously all those things. But think of the Mafia (so-called) as it was originally organized and operated on the Sicilian home island. The Binh Xuyen were our neighbors. We knew their names and reputations just as people today are familiar with the names and particulars of popular entertainers and sports figures. They were inescapably part of our lives, sometimes even our benefactors when they occasionally cultivated a Robin Hood image.

Although the original, very complicated gang roots may have involved piracy, labor racketeering, and "protection insurance" schemes, during World War II the leadership, in tune with broad national sentiment, assumed an anti-colonial identity, and the Binh Xuyen name was specifically adopted in 1945. Alliance with southern communists and other nationalists echoed a theme in Asian history wherein bandit chieftains might metamorphose into patriots. Binh Xuyen attacking the French, followed by French counterattacks, during late 1945 through 1946 were the root cause of insecurity in Saigon and surrounding districts; that was the specific reason for our family and many others to have sought safety in the provinces.

Failure to defeat the reinforcing French Union forces caused a shaking out of gang leadership in 1946 and a splitting away from a functional alliance with the communist party. A free agent again, "godfather" Le Van Vien, better known as "Bay Vien," made a convenient deal with the ascendant-returning French colonial authorities. The arrangement ceded policing authority in the Cho Lon–Khanh Hoi–Nha Be area to the Binh Xuyen in return for Bay Vien's commitment to exterminate Saigon-area Viet Minh. He could substantially fulfill that promise because of his previous intimate familiarity with local communist leaders when cooperating with them. Absent competition, and licensed by Emperor Bao Dai with French acquiescence, the Binh Xuyen drew income from nightclubs, casinos, and dance halls. Divorced of nationalist political motivation, the organization became entirely criminal, spinning off into the evilest forms of exploitive opium trafficking and forced prostitution.

Still, they were so rooted into Cho Lon–Khanh Hoi, and some other Saigon neighborhoods, that despite awareness and fear of what the Binh Xuyen had become, the gang could not be ignored. Twice while I was a young teenager, I was invited—therefore required as though requisitioned—to entertain at a gathering of Bay Vien family members and loyal supporters. Refusal was not an option. I had to sit with the leader and his friends, smiling as though having no cares at all and pleased to be in the company of thieves and worse. Mother and Father were afraid for me and for themselves. We sometimes talked about moving from our neighborhood to a district on the other side of Saigon where Binh Xuyen presence and control were not so strong. But we knew it was unwise to share our thoughts with others.

I continued singing and dancing, earning small amounts of money for our family, but when not performing for an audience it pleased me to be alone, to write, to draw pictures that amused my aunt and her friends, and to dream of someday having a special someone with whom I would share a perfect love. There was nothing sexual about that vision. I certainly understood from the attention paid to me that there was something attractive about my appearance, but this seemed insignificant to me. Even though performing was more enjoyable than school, I knew that it was important to focus on doing well in my classes first and foremost, and my favorite studies were always writing and art.

The only consequential man for me in those years was Father, and we did not understand each other at all. I gradually became aware that he frequently betrayed my mother with other women, even stealing from the household accounts and Mother's purse to buy affection elsewhere. Once, when I was still a child, soon after we returned to Saigon from Tra Vinh, he asked me where Mother kept her jewelry. He promised candy if I could show him. Unfortunately, I did know my mother's hiding place, and I wanted that candy. When Mother found out that she had been robbed by her own husband so that he could entice other women, she simply held me close while crying, forgiving my innocent candy-motivated betrayal. Father, angry because I told Mother what he had done, yelled loudly, broke furniture, and threw away family photographs. My mother collapsed, bleeding from mouth and nose. I knew, vaguely, that some men were accustomed to behaving meanly, but I could not understand how my own father could hurt the woman who, after all, had twice saved his life.

My father often beat me when I was little, sometimes while holding my hair and wielding a bamboo stick. I would grit my teeth and not cry out. I even cut my hair short, almost like a boy, so that he could not easily grip me. He took that as a challenge and began to strike me whenever he was drunk or dissatisfied. When he spoke with me it was almost always belligerently. I would frequently flee to friendly neighbors' homes where kind auntie figures would soothe and protect me. Looking back, still painfully, I think Father was starting to resent my beginning to provide more income for the family than he could, and so somehow felt that I needed to be controlled. My regard for him was eroded by his continual betrayal of my mother and fear and resentment of occasional rages when he would hit me with fist or stick.

Outside of my tragic family circle there were significant historic changes in Viet Nam. In 1954, France lost her Indo-China colonies. French administrators, police, and military for years had been pushing their way around Saigon with, aside from a few assassinations and local attacks, general impunity. Vietnamese had to accommodate. However, some joined the Viet Minh, either leaving the city for remote base areas or remaining in Saigon as secret agents. Many families encouraged a relative to work for the French so as to have an "ear" on the inside. One of my father's brothers worked for the French security service, headquartered on upper Catinat Street, and he brought home frightening tales of what happened during French interrogations of Vietnamese "suspects." Occasionally, a survivor, turned reluctant informer, would be led into our neighborhood, face covered by a burlap rice-bag mask, to point out other supposed opponents of French rule who, if present, would be immediately seized. We all feared the very name "Catinat."

But the French grip on our country was increasingly tenuous. Viet Minh divisions defeated French battalions in the far northern Dien Bien Phu valley. And elsewhere in that part of our country, communists were generally taking the offensive. At Kontum and An Khe in the central highlands, French Union soldiers were forced to abandon their positions. An uneasy, not really satisfactory (for the contesting parties), compromise during the 1954 peace conference in Geneva required regrouping of communist military units to the northern part of Viet Nam and allowed the movement of hundreds of thousands of Vietnamese, mostly Catholic, from the north to the south. There could be elections two years later, supposedly, for uniting north and south, although election procedures were not clear. But French rule over our country was definitely finished.

It seemed to many Vietnamese that there might be an opportunity for some alternative to the communist-shaped and -controlled liberation army forces. Much, maybe most, of the Viet Minh energy had emerged from general nationalism and a vigorous anti-colonial crusade. The French finally, awkwardly, and clumsily were going to leave. As they began shuffling towards the exit, other foreign visitors knocked on our door. Calling themselves "Americans" and arriving from the USA, a country little known by the Vietnamese, they would be like new guests at our family table. We hoped they would not carve Viet Nam further apart but instead act as a counterweight against imposition of a one-party Viet Minh government. Our conflict-weary tendency, even for a curious teenage girl like myself, was hopefully optimistic. And the Americans did obtain some credit for bringing a nationalist, Ngo Dinh Diem, back to Viet Nam in mid-1954 to be appointed prime minister by Emperor Bao Dai, even though most of us in the south did not know much about him and his family.

Saigon was in a state of confusion during late 1954. The French were departing but obviously resented the appearance of replacement by Americans. Vietnamese who previously depended on

French favor were vulnerable, and some prepared to follow their masters to Europe. The newly installed prime minister Diem was determined to organize and preside over a strong central government rather than play a balancing role between regional entities that were previously allowed local autonomy in return for acknowledging colonial and Bao Dai royal legitimacy. The French, even though defeated, attempted to position themselves for retaining commercial and political influence.

The least reputable and so most immediately vulnerable of their southern allies was our local, and frankly criminal, Binh Xuyen gang. When Prime Minister Diem ordered an attack on the Binh Xuyen enterprises and their so-called police a few months later, many Vietnamese were doubtful that he would succeed. The French sought to use Emperor Bao Dai, then sporting abroad on the Riviera, to arrange replacement of the prime minister by a puppet of their own creation and selection. It seemed that all players on our national stage, even the Americans, were hesitating, not sure how the balance of power might shift in Saigon's military barracks.

But for all the criticism mustered against him in later years, Ngo Dinh Diem, at this point in our history, was correct and decisive. He ordered the Viet Nam armed forces to attack the Binh Xuyen and eliminate armed non-government forces in the capital city. The military, and especially paratroopers, supported Prime Minister Diem. The Cao Dai religious military leader, Trinh Minh The, brought his soldiers southeast from their Tay Ninh stronghold to cooperate with the national army. Not many Binh Xuyen survived. A few jumped the wall bordering one of their compounds and the neighborhood cemetery, then escaped through our backyard. One man was badly wounded, intestines visible, and a visiting aunt positioned a shallow bowl over his stomach area and bound it in place with a long piece of toweling. He shuffled away, but I could not imagine how he might survive. Some others may have escaped through Vinh Hoi and Khanh Hoi, and then across the Saigon River.

A few Binh Xuyen were later rumored to have joined remnant Viet Minh forces beyond Bien Hoa, although it is doubtful that communists would trust those same bandits who betrayed them several years earlier. And I also think that any Viet Minh remaining in the south were then keeping a low profile while waiting to see what might happen in the aftermath of the Geneva Agreements and French withdrawal. Bay Vien himself slithered away to France, but his son and other key supporters were captured. Political and military leaders frequently describe the elimination of opponents as executions, but there were no trials for the captive Binh Xuyen. They were simply murdered one by one, just as they had previously murdered others.

Trinh Minh The, the Cao Dai general who rallied to support the prime minister, was killed during the fighting in Saigon. The circumstances were thought by everyone in our neighborhood to be mysterious because he was not at the center of battle. Whatever really happened, his exit from this world did in fact reduce the list of political-military actors who might someday oppose the newly triumphant prime minister. An important bridge in Saigon–Cho Lon was renamed in honor of Trinh Minh The, but thereafter, over time, the man was forgotten.

Another major dissident force in the southern part of our country were the Hoa Hao Buddhist congregations. Somewhat like the Binh Xuyen, this militant Buddhist group had a history of fracture with different components sometimes opposed to the French and occasionally making local arrangements with them. However, Hoa Hao believers were also consistently anti-communist because their teacher, Huynh Phu So, was ambushed and disappeared, probably killed, in 1947 after refusing to conglomerate with the Viet Minh. Now, since the Binh Xuyen were eliminated and the Cao Dai had been brought more or less within the government embrace, President Diem ordered the army to move against Hoa Hao groups in the Mekong area. In about a year, the Hoa Hao forces were generally defeated, fleeing to swamps or their Seven Mountains lair near Cambodia. As with the Binh Xuyen, so now Hoa Hao leaders were collected for prison or execution. One, Ba Cut, was guillotined in a grim echo of the disgraceful French colonial practice.

CHAPTER 3

Young Mother

I n spring 1955, a birthday, my sixteenth, launched me into a life-altering year. A young student from Hue, the primary city of Central Viet Nam and former imperial capital, was introduced to my parents as a potential boarder beginning in August. Those of our church who recommended the boy described him as the son of a prosperous merchant, graduate of the best school in Hue, and seriously committed to advanced study in Saigon. Mother and Father agreed to accept him. They thought there could even be a benefit from my circumstantial association with someone close in age, someone who was serious, compared to other young men and women whom I was encountering in clubs and restaurants.

I was immediately attracted to the young student, not many years older than I, who boarded in our house. I looked forward to seeing and spending time with him when I returned home from school, a music lesson, or a singing engagement. Sometimes we even shared the family table to study. We took walks together and did some street shopping for fun in Saigon and Cho Lon. At the beginning, there wasn't anything romantic about our growing attachment. It was only as though we both needed a companion, a confidant. He was always interested in my stories of what was seen and experienced among entertainers. I loved hearing about his studies and the future that he believed would be built upon an already successful family business. Glancing backward, now decades past, I realize our relationship was becoming circumstantially emotional even though absent of physical intimacy. But danger hovered all around because we were too often alone in the house, and privacy allowed hand-holding and sitting together more closely than we ought to have.

One day, while I was napping in my room, he entered and lay down with me. For the first time, and only that one time, we embraced each other while skin touched skin. Clumsily, betraying his own inexperience, he placed his penis between my legs for his own enjoyment of a physical feeling that, at the same time, also provided some satisfaction of my own curiosity. The liveliness and growth, the insistence with which his maleness responded, amazed me. He promised to take care not to penetrate. I was not sure what that meant, having only a faded image of what seemed to have been done to my cousin in Tra Vinh. But surely this pleasuring with him was totally different. I had promised myself not to make the same mistake that many young girls, young women, would when alone with a boyfriend. But now, there I was, ready and willingly seduced by an intense young love.

We both understood the prime necessity for being careful, that I should absolutely never be pregnant until he could speak with his family. So, my first lover's promise on that initial occasion, to refrain from deeply penetrating, to avoid depositing within me, was, we thought, sufficient to maintain the necessary appearance of innocence. But the liveliness, the very evolutionary essence of sperm within the male coital liquid, is to swim upstream, surmount obstacles, and thereby stimulate new life. Love may not conquer all, but sperm frequently will. At first, I was so childishly uninformed that I did not even know how a woman's body responds to the beginning of life within. I missed a period, and then another just before Christmas. I was naive but knew enough to be alarmed. I could not long obscure my nervous state of mind from Mother. So, surprisingly, aggravatingly for my mother and father, and with eventual shock to the family of my student-lover, I was at the beginning of 1956, and after only once having lain with the boy, at less than 17 years of age, pregnant!

Making matters much worse for me, and my parents, was the absence of the young man. He had returned to Hue in December for a brief stint working in the family business, and while far from me was persuaded to accept an arranged marriage pressed upon him by his father and another well-connected family. He accepted, even while unaware of my pregnancy. Our dream when he had studied in Saigon, and while we would ponder how to arrange a future beyond the one-time intimacy on my bed, had usually been imagining we could continue as we were while he finished his studies and then somehow draw both families into our own circle of acceptance and happiness. Now reality shattered illusion. The young man was back at home, caught in a web from which he could not escape. He never returned to Saigon or to me.

Father was angry! He was angry with the young man, feeling deceived by his lodger, but even more furious with me, thinking himself betrayed by his foolish daughter. Mother was more sympathetic, perhaps older woman to younger woman; but at the same time, she seemed to reproach herself for not having foreseen the possibility of temptation between two young people too frequently unsupervised and unobserved and with time, lots of time, for each other.

Father, anticipating ridicule from the neighbors and shame for himself, kicked me out of our home. For several days I had to hide in an outbuilding to the far rear of our property, sleep under old rice bags, and subsist on scraps that Mother would smuggle to me when she could. Occasionally, a kind old woman neighbor would pass me fruit from her home garden. I wandered nearby streets, sometimes overcome with tears, often hungry as never before. I would stand outside a soup shop, smelling *pho,* our Vietnamese beef broth, and then turn away due to not having even one piaster in my pocket. I was effectively homeless. Since those lonely days I have never lacked sympathy for others who, for whatever reason, are deprived of a roof and something to eat. Finally, my mother convinced Father to allow me back into our house to sit at the family table. But day after day, he barely spoke to me, and I think that only by his awareness of my carrying another life did I escape frequent, if not constant, beatings.

I was desperate to save myself from miserable confinement and constant haranguing from Father, and I had built a strong self-image based on my own achievements. So, because my pregnancy was not yet apparent at a casual glance, I began to sing again in a few local clubs. Providing income for the family soothed father's anger, although I always gave my piasters to Mother, hoping that she would be able to save as much as possible.

After only a month, desperately wanting some separation from the miserable circumstances at home and overhearing political conversation in restaurants and therefore aware of change in my country, I thought it perhaps possible to be a small part of the nascent southern regional patriotism by attaching myself to a cause above and beyond artistic performance. Serious personal commitment could salvage the reputation of family and myself in our immediate neighborhood, while simultaneously building a respectable independent personal identity. I knew, vaguely and with absent detail, that a new Special Office for Civic Action had already been organized during the previous year. It was responsible for providing information about our Saigon government to people living in the districts and hamlets. Rural families, it was thought, by being better informed would support a noncommunist government. Every civic action-team operation included a drama and entertainment component to accompany the information cadre that specialized in organizational work and propaganda. Energetic reaching into hamlets, and even working in Saigon neighborhoods, had already delivered the 1955 referendum votes that changed the form of government to a republic, effectively deposing Emperor Bao Dai in favor of Ngo Dinh Diem, who would make himself president.

A friend from our church enquired and told me that a southerner, Kieu Cong Cung, a former Viet Minh, had provided the concept and organizational plan for civic action to then prime minister, now president, Ngo Dinh Diem. Cung was thought controversial by some Catholics because of his Viet Minh background, but he was also believed to be honest, and it was generally known that Diem trusted him. So, with reluctant family acquiescence, I joined what was called Cong Dan Vu, or Dan Su Vu, and went forth on political action missions in the countryside.

Our dance and song performances in province capitals and district towns, mixed with political exhortation, were usually held in temporarily converted government buildings. But in hamlets and villages, a stage was fashioned of crude wood with palm-frond sides and backing. If there would be a stage curtain at all, it was simply one sheet of old linen opened and closed manually by the entertainers. We were welcomed everywhere because people were desperate for diversion, and there was in fact considerable curiosity about the new government. Our performances, even though awfully amateur, excited both young and old.

One of the principal messages delivered by our information cadre was to call upon former Viet Minh resistance activists and fighters to identify themselves for registration with village and district offices. I very naively believed, at the beginning of my service in early 1956, that the purpose was to recognize anti-colonial patriots and prevent false accusations of banditry against them. So thinking, I was puzzled that most families were generally unresponsive to our message for identification, and on a few occasions our loudspeakers attracted a little, perhaps just symbolic, gunfire. Frightened when that happened, I supposed it was just confusion born from the newness of national independence that would eventually be clarified.

Working in the provinces and hamlets revived memories of my brief childhood in Tra Vinh. I could see that rural people in every province were poor, but they were generous in sharing what little they had among themselves and with visitors. They were still suffering from the impact of fifteen years of conflict followed by some inconsistencies on the part of a new government still organizing itself.

Weeks passed quickly. As we moved in and out of provinces, even while excited by the work I was beginning to suffer the physical effects of the sixth and seventh months of pregnancy. Weight gain, extreme discomfort, and a youthful ignorance of the changes occurring within me combined to require my return home. Mother buffered me from the paternal temper and began to accompany me on slow daily walks around the neighborhood. She counseled perseverance, endurance, and acceptance of the pain that is inescapably part of the burden borne by all women bringing forth new life.

My first child, Nguyen Thi Le Thu (autumn tears), was delivered in a Saigon hospital on August 20, 1956, after almost a full day of agony, when I was little more than seventeen. Her birth certificate lists my occupation as "government civic action cadre." The nurses had previously informed Mother, in some amazement, that during a prenatal examination my vaginal veil had still been intact. So, this was a virgin birth, they believed, and perhaps one with spiritual significance. But you and I understand, dear reader, sharing a knowledge of anatomy and the feverish movement of those little rascals in the male fluid, that apparent miraculous procreation is not deity dependent. Heavenly or not, from her first breath Le Thu was weak and struggled for air. I could not leave her side for months, and she would need specialized medical attention and treatment for several years. In fact, in 1970 and 1971, Le Thu as a teenager required treatment at Grall Hospital, including months in a plaster body cast.

A few weeks after Le Thu was born, the father of my absent student boyfriend visited our family in Saigon. He was a "hard head."

He refused to even consider any possibility of my having a relationship with his own supposed noble lineage, probably fearing I'd potentially lay a hand on his successful fish sauce condiment commercial enterprise. The sole concession, he said, was to offer his son a conditional choice: The boy would be allowed to recognize our daughter, but if my student (as I still thought of him) chose to do that, he would be entirely cut off from his own family.

How lenient! That tiny concession, really a mean-spirited dictate, angered my mother and father since it so clearly demonstrated disrespect for our southern family. Perhaps from a sense of shame, some slight acknowledgment of his own family responsibility, the visitor offered me a packet of money. Whether that might have been arrogant presumption to buy us off or salve for his own personal but well disguised feeling of shame, I do not know. But for my own part, there was no way that I would bow or beg for his reconsideration. I could never take any amount of insultingly proffered money as equivalent value for my daughter. So, I pressed the money back into the old man's hands. I would not allow him—and he should have known better than—to insult me and my family by placing a price on a life that he considered an inconvenience for himself. My own father, usually avaricious, told him to keep his money and leave.

While at home, at first enduring the final months of pregnancy and later while caring for Le Thu, I completed secondary school. My mother was a capable caring angel for her granddaughter. Le Thu, with intensive medical attention, was improving, and so it was again possible to begin singing in a few restaurants and provide income to offset expenses. But I missed the sense of adventure and independence previously experienced with civic action. So, with family agreement I rejoined the government cadre program and once again went forth on missions in the countryside.

I was immediately sensitive to the early 1957 differences, greater than before, between Saigon and the provinces. People in the capital were beginning to dress well, appearing relatively affluent and shopping along the downtown main streets. But the trickle of foreign assistance and the commodity imports making that circumstance possible did not appear to have any effect in our poor rural countryside. In Central Viet Nam, people rooted in their hamlets were uniformly poor compared to those in the far south. They seemed less well fed. Clothing was patched and threadbare. People attending our cultural performances in Binh Dinh, Quang Ngai, and Quang Tri were so desperate, so unhappy, compared to audiences in other provinces that I was moved to give most of my own clothes and as much money as I could spare to women who approached me after performances.

My traveling valise was quickly emptied, and my personal shoulder bag thinned. I needed to buy some things in the next good-sized market town but had barely any money left. The manager of our troupe noticed and offered money if I would favor him with the loan of my body while traveling. Once before in Saigon, after an entertainment arranged for President Diem, I was groped by a senior leader and solved that situation by complaining directly to Kieu Cong Cung. Now, even though far from the capital and that especially ethical leader, I was not at all disposed to be importuned into the clutches of the dirty escorting official. Fortunately, sympathetic fellow entertainers noticed, made a collection among themselves, and loaned me enough money to last until our group returned to Saigon.

All civic action missions into the Central Highlands, if intended to connect with one of the hill tribes, presented a special set of difficulties. The language difference was profound. At that time, more than sixty years past, few Vietnamese could speak Rhade, Jarai, Bahnar, Sedang, or any of the other tribal languages. This was not just a problem of regional dialect, like between Northern and Southern Vietnamese, but a deep gulf between our tonal language and those non-tonal ones having Khmer or Malay roots. It was possible to speak French with some tribal leaders who could then translate our message to their people, but it seemed awkward to be working through the former colonial language to convey newly independent political content.

There were always important political differences between ethnic Vietnamese and tribespeople in the Central Viet Nam highlands, much like the tension between Cambodians and Vietnamese in the Mekong provinces. The basic problem was about land ownership and land use, complicated by Vietnamese ethnic prejudice and corresponding tribal resentment. French colonialists previously administered the hill and plateau area separately from their other divisions of our country. They claimed that doing so was for the purpose of protecting tribal lands and rights, but the true intent was to guarantee themselves primacy in exploiting resources and opening plantations. After the general, but not complete, departure of French business enterprises, our new government opened the highlands to Vietnamese commercial interests and settlement. This was especially beneficial for the 1954 refugees from northern Viet Nam, but further aggravated Vietnamese relations with tribes accustomed to theoretical primacy in their homelands.

In February 1957, a cultural group was selected to accompany President Diem and officials on a ceremonial visit to Banmethuot, the principal town within the Rhade tribal area. The presidential party flew in on a special plane. All cultural performers and an information service film crew were placed on a separate C-47 (usually a troop carrier), with two long rows of uncomfortable canvas webbed benches but with good space between for musical instruments and cameras. We singers and dancers were told to wear what was supposed to be an approximation, to the Vietnamese eye, of tribal dress. On the flight northward I wondered what Rhade folk attending the ceremony in Banmethuot might think of us. Would they be flattered, offended, amused, or so inured to disparagement that our costumes would be only one more insult among many, and so simply ignored?

My speculative thoughts were interrupted by our old aircraft landing just prior to the one carrying President Diem. We immediately proceeded to the ceremonial site so that our Saigon troupe could stage a colorful welcome for the president and his party. Dressed as instructed, we would appear on the national newsreel to be enthusiastic tribal citizens. But as the first to arrive, we entertainers were greeted by real Rhade playing a repetitive but melodious tune on bronze gongs of different sizes, a sound something like water rushing downstream tumbling over boulders.

We quickly arranged ourselves in order of appearance and performance and moved forward as the president and others arrived. We greeted him, all around in a sort of circle, and I remember thinking to myself that President Diem had a warm and friendly appearance. Suddenly a man, Vietnamese I am sure, drew a pistol and shot at the president. Unexpectedly, we singers and dancers were his shield, bodyguards in effect! There was instantaneous confusion, yells, shrill screaming, but the presidential guards reacted fairly quickly and, moving through our circle of amateurs, gripped the president and moved him away. President Diem was unharmed, but an official accompanying him was wounded. The remainder of the scheduled program was cancelled, and everyone was brought to the airfield for immediate return to Saigon.

I knew the president was not entirely popular. Suppressing the Binh Xuyen gang earned him much respect, especially in Saigon, and he was applauded for having done so. Organizing the 1955 referendum to dissolve rule by Emperor Bao Dai and announcing a republican form of government was welcomed. But he gave an impression of remoteness, and retaining the Bao Dai/French puppet government flag without considering the alternatives appeared to some as an incomplete break from the past.

He soon thereafter visited America at the invitation of President Eisenhower. That gesture of American support was significant for Vietnamese who were committed to an identity separate from the northern and now communist part of our country. The central issue for many of us, even me, was whether any leader could realistically appeal to all, or at least most, of the disparate groups in a newly forming country. President Diem did provide firm, even forceful, leadership. He "jump-started" the country, but some critics asserted that the "jumping" had mostly been suppression of those thought to be opponents or potential opponents. Some of his family members, especially two brothers, Nhu and Can, were controversial, even disliked, because although not elected to any position, they wielded influence to an extent that was almost determinative authority. As for me, well, I was still in shock, numb several weeks, for having been so close to the Banmethuot attempted assassination.

I was not even slightly politically connected, but I was living and working within a politicizing society, listening to everyone around me, sensitive to conditions and opinions in Saigon and, more important, had just recently been observant of some provinces and hamlets. It seemed to me that the intent and emphasis of rural work initiated by President Diem and Kieu Cong Cung changed considerably during late 1956 while I had been at home.

Earlier, when the civic action program supported the national referendum to approve establishing a republic in place of imperial rule, in effect deposing Emperor Bao Dai, my family and most acquaintances did not consider that step in any way wrong. Who would not want to push a playboy emperor off the stage? I knew identification of former Viet Minh was required within our earlier tasking but had not understood that those self-acknowledged or accused were almost always later arrested. Now, through the remainder of 1957 and into 1958, I sensed the civic action program of which I had been a small part but that was a large part of my life was changing and becoming more agitational than informational. The shift of focus was further complicated by our Vietnamese regional and societal differences.

Participating in civic action and performing for military units relieved some of the tension of being a young unmarried mother.

At the start of Cong Dan Vu, the government understandably wanted assurance that everyone dispatched to attract rural support would be completely loyal to the new government. Inducting northern refugees fleeing communist rule, recently arrived in the south and mostly Catholic by faith, appeared a probable guarantee of loyalty. But later, we southerners realized that the preponderance of northerners would self-perpetuate. Being Catholic myself, I did not consider religious identity a problem. But the northern and southern language dialects, not just pronunciation but including cultural referents, are very different. Sometimes communication between people from Sa Dec (south) and Hoa Binh (north), even with mutual goodwill, can be confusing. And goodwill between grim northerners who had abandoned property and family, and we southerners who might feel the need to protect family members who may have been Viet Minh combatants, was often lacking.

There were two kinds of civic action field assignments. The easiest was to accompany senior government representatives on visits to a military region or province and provide official entertainment. The other, and more important, we called *cong tac dac biet*—that is, "special mission." Special missions brought us into hamlets where we would be part of an operation calling upon people to affirm loyalty to the government and, increasingly, denounce communists. I sensed that civic action was becoming, much more than in the past, an instrument for denunciation and intimidation rather than making the case for supporting our republic. Civic action leaders in the field were behaving as though their only duty was to identify people who were unfriendly toward our government. We were failing to recognize that without presenting a persuasive description of policies and without delivery of the benefits derived from those policies, poor farm families would not be motivated to risk their lives by aligning with our new government.

Although unsure of what might constitute relevant political concerns, I was beginning to think critically, to have questions. I thought that, while I was only a simple entertainer, dancer, and singer of songs, and still very young, I might have an opportunity to express my thoughts to Kieu Cong Cung, who was also a southerner, had always been friendly, and behaved respectably. But he was too soon frequently ill, retired to his home, and died a couple of years later. Without any way to register my views, and wary of being thought disloyal, I simply decided that from that point forward I would not take any more special missions into hamlets and would only perform for official events when polite refusal would be awkward. I would have more time available to perform in Saigon nightclubs and restaurants, build my reputation, and draw sufficient income to help my family. I would be able to care for Le Thu and more easily pay medical expenses resulting from her ongoing treatment at Gralle Hospital.

Le Thu was always ill, weak, and listless as a baby and even at this time, although more than two years old and receiving intensive care from my mother and me, still lacked the energy typically displayed by "the terrible twos." She was seen and treated in the best, and very expensive, foreign hospitals in Saigon. She appeared constantly malnourished by usually presenting a swollen belly and thin limbs. Continuing evaluation and tests finally resulted in a diagnosis of digestive and urinary tract irregularities complicated by skeletal weakness of the spine. The next six years of her life were full of pain. Surgery and a body cast were endured by Le Thu and paid by me, emotionally as well as financially. My mother was a constant angel, caring for Le Thu while I sang by night to earn the money that we needed.

A Viet Nam film industry, with relatively small companies compared to developments in Hong Kong, was evolving. I was a featured performer at age seventeen, although not a lead actress, in *Nguoi Dep Binh Duong* (Binh Duong Beauty) released in 1957. I portrayed a rather evil character, which was so uncomfortable for me I decided to avoid film in the future.

I did wonder, from time to time, how different my life might have been if the romance with my student boyfriend had proceeded from innocent dalliance to commitment. When I was persuaded to take part in a Kim Cuong theatrical and musical troupe visit to Hue, an opportunity was afforded for a final meeting with Le Thu's father. It was a sort of testing the degree of residual sentiment for both of us. We arranged to meet at his family's business office. It was an emotional reunion in a stark environment. We spoke of what might have been. He was now willing, he told me, to give up a future with his own family and the family fortune. But I told him that could not be a workable solution because he was already obligated to marry another woman; moreover, if he broke away from his family, deep regret would certainly follow, and he would later resent me and Le Thu. "We must abandon the past," I told him. He persuaded me to exchange a kiss in memory of our young love, but I felt an emotional vacuum in my own heart and so told him that we absolutely could never have any kind of continuing relationship. We parted the next morning so that I could return to Saigon with my friends, and we never met again.

Ngo Dinh Diem was our self-made president for the south of Viet Nam. His family provided him more than just emotional comfort. Brother (and bishop, subsequently archbishop) Thuc exercised broad influence over any subject of interest to himself. Brother Can was granted a kind of viceroy status in the traditional Hue region. Brother Nhu organized government employees and other politically interested people into a broad-based Phong Trao Cach Mang Quoc Gia (National Revolutionary Movement) within which a secretive political party, Can Lao Nhan Vi Cach Mang Dang (Revolutionary Personalist Labor Party) served as the backbone and enforcement mechanism. Both organizations, in our national tradition, were almost entirely male. But Tran Le Xuan, wife of brother Nhu, eventually organized a corresponding, and somewhat countervailing, Women's Solidarity Movement that was supportive of President

Diem but also assertive of feminine interests as she understood and defined them.

Although still awfully young, I had survived violence while a child and witnessed rural problems that communists could exploit. When Ngo Dinh Diem announced that the southern Republic of Viet Nam would not participate in the elections that foreigners, at Geneva in 1954, imagined for 1956, it was obvious that we would, at least for a long time, have a divided country. The young Republic of Viet Nam would need an army prepared to defend a separate southern identity.

CHAPTER 4

Arranged Marriage

The most conspicuous difficulty for President Diem was that, as with civil administrators and police, in the near term he would be depending on military officers, who were previously part of the French Colonial Army. Their numbers included a few who were habitual exploiters of any situation for personal advantage. There were certainly better men at junior grades, but even there, French command, authority, and personnel practice had been pervasive and corrosive. Having inherited their position and rank from the defeated and departing colonial power, too many of the newly elevated colonels and generals, even some younger Vietnamese officers, strutted like peacocks in uniforms adorned with fine French and Bao Dai medals that were awarded for recently killing other Vietnamese.

I thought we needed time to school and test in action a new generation of civil and military leaders sworn to protect the south. Meanwhile, the president would need to be watchful of those he placed in command, evaluating their performance in terms of competence and willingness to sacrifice for more than their own interest.

I had my own real problems. Having naively thought that being a mother would serve as a protection, I learned instead that some men believe that a young woman with a child but no husband signifies

An exceptionally small waist emphasized a curvaceous body and was basic to contracts for advertising and subsequent film publicity.

exploitable vulnerability and availability. Moreover, at that time in Saigon I was cultivating a certain daring image to differentiate myself from other entertainers. In the heady atmosphere of newly free Saigon, there were so many young women competing to be advertising models, to have contracts for singing, to appear on stage, that I had to be imaginative in order to hold an edge. I was already the first to curl my hair, thereby adopting an exotic (from the Vietnamese perspective) international appearance. Now I was the first to wear swimsuits, even a semi-bikini, for popular magazines and billboard advertising. Clients knew that remarkable breasts coupled with an unusually small waist attracted the eye.

And yet, I was still an innocent at heart, and so potentially exploitable by sly others. I remember agreeing to pose for a soft drink photo advertisement with no suspicion of sexual insinuation. Days later, one of my singer girlfriends whispered in my ear that the placement of the bottle in the widely distributed photograph had a *duong vat* (phallic) intimation. I did not know what she meant, what that could have to do with a bottle of cola, until she explained the image to me. Thereafter I was much more attentive to how photographers would pose me for an advertising client.

Singing in nightclubs around the capital, going from one spot to another by taxi or sometimes by cyclo (our beloved three-wheeled pedicab), was my fundamental source of income, and it kept my image before the public in a way that made my inclusion in commercial advertising good business for some companies. Frequently, men followed to press upon an escorting family member some gift, jewelry or money enclosed in an envelope, hoping to earn favor. My mother would collect all tribute and hold it, as far as possible from my father, in safe keeping. Although terribly young, not yet twenty, I adopted a smiling pose, an air of serenity that was at the same time strangely remote from the immediate surroundings, so that, gradually, the "fan base" understood I would always be ultimately inaccessible. Occasionally, I would be away from Saigon for a few days while participating in an official government-sponsored program of entertainment, frequently for the Cong Binh (engineers) or Bao An (civil guard command).

Saigon in those first years of independence was a lively attractive city without the aristocratic pretension of Hue or grimness of communist Hanoi. Whereas Hue was of the last dynasty and suffused with feudal pride, and Hanoi's twisting narrow streets concealed simmering discontent, my city of birth boasted wide boulevards shaded by tall trees. I must reluctantly allow departed colonialists credit for the quality of their municipal planning. Still, it seemed to me that more than anything, it was nature's abundant rainfall and our mild southern winters that provided Saigon with comparative beauty. Year-round green trees and flowering shrubs contrasted with the drabness of the colder north. Even the most modest of small Vietnamese homes could tend beautiful plants and small plots for the spices important to our home cooking. Vietnamese who took possession of previous French properties might now even have private semi-tropical gardens, and there were a few compounds with swimming pools!

Based on rice exports and, much later, French rubber, coffee, and tea plantation companies, Saigon had developed a vibrant commercial atmosphere for more than a hundred years. More than any other urban center in Viet Nam, Saigon enjoyed something of an international atmosphere because European, not just French, companies were accustomed to commercial trade for Vietnamese products. Japanese buyers sought out our lacquer trees to export resin to their country as an essential ingredient for their traditional handicrafts. I was told that even the sands from Cam Ranh Bay had some commercial value.

Beginning in the late 1950s, Americans were seen more and more on the streets of Saigon. And their allies, especially from the Philippines, were also there with increasing frequency immediately after the French military went home. Following the 1957 visit of President Diem to America, the number of American advisors providing training and equipment delivery increased. Some Americans, Vietnamese officers told me, were even in the military headquarters, almost as though they worked there! I recall that the general impression of those early Americans, on the part of most Vietnamese, was favorable. Their behavior was informal and friendly, in nice contrast to French colonial officials and soldiers, and there were still not too many of the newcomers.

Although I was much less frequently in the provinces, friends were telling me security was deteriorating in many districts where the Viet Minh had previously been most active against the French. President Diem had already decided that the southern region–based Republic of Viet Nam would not take part in the 1956 national elections suggested in Geneva by foreigners. It was a wise decision, even though that announcement guaranteed an early revival of communist political activity and military action. I am sure communist party leaders would have eventually called for insurrection, but no matter how spurious, communists could now claim there was no alternative path for uniting North and South. And I wondered if the identification and denunciation campaigns might have alienated a few people in hamlets to some new level of frustration. Desperate people are susceptible to persuasion by others who meretriciously advocate revenge. I did not want to dwell on those thoughts because I had so recently, albeit only as a civic action entertainer, been circumstantially involved.

I had my own continuing difficulty. The new class of senior military officers, generals, and colonels, perhaps aping French predecessors or just exhibiting base male primate behavior, looked upon entertainers as women who ought to be thrilled to accept their company. The worst among them, a strutting boastful bantam, was Ton That Dinh, who often hosted entertainment spectaculars at his military command headquarters in Pleiku from 1958 onward.[1] He would ask that a national troupe of instrumentalists and singers be made available to perform for soldiers in morale-building performances. Those selected would be required to travel on the C-47 assigned to Dinh, and he would frequently be on the aircraft when

---

[1] Ton That Dinh was member of a Hue family previously affiliated with the last royal family. The "Ton That" family is so widespread and complex that frequently one member will not know or even have heard of another. General Dinh, who commanded the military region surrounding Saigon, was a key figure among the conspirators who toppled the first Republic of Viet Nam and murdered President Diem in 1963. Dinh was born in Hue in 1927 and died in California in 2013.

it arrived in Saigon to pick up the performers. He would habitually ask one of the girls to sit with him. I always pleaded fatigue and refused, because his customary behavior, groping and making lewd remarks, was so offensive.

Once, after an evening performance in Banmethuot, Dinh demanded that I remain after the other entertainers departed to return to the hotel. I insisted that another girl stay with me. Dinh attempted to separate us, but I gripped my friend's *ao dai* so tightly, it was as though we were chained together. Muttering curses, Dinh had no alternative but to drive us in his jeep to our hotel, in an ugly mood all the way.

Ton That Dinh's rude behavior and presumption of romantic privilege was not limited to his remote area of command. He was a frequent Saigon visitor to advance one scheme or another, or just to make an appearance in theaters and nightclubs whenever the mood suited him. Once he placed himself at a table just in front of the musicians, laid his pistol on the table, and demanded that I take the stage to sing his favorite songs. On another occasion, Dinh ordered a junior officer to find my home and insist that I go to his Saigon residence for games, to play cards, and God knows what else. I refused, and Mother and Father placed themselves at my side and told the frustrated bearer of the invitation to leave our house.

I was particularly saddened by the ongoing Dinh travesty because it was generally assumed that he had converted to Catholicism to curry favor with the president. The apparent success of that trick—the acquiescence of the president to raise a stubby boy general—caused me to question the president's perception of those he trusted to protect the nation and safeguard his own life. Moreover, my father had no appetite, or even patience, for what seemed to be the constant struggle to protect me from importuning government officers, of whom Dinh was the worst yet not the sole offender. With Mother's agreement, my father decided, and then persuaded me, that I needed to marry in order to have the benefit of moral and social protection by law.

The owners of several clubs and restaurants asked my parents for approval to marry me, but many of those businessmen were also notorious womanizers; although my father had his own failings in that respect, he would not accept the same behavior from a son-in-law. Amorous and marital interest was expressed by some wealthy merchants for whose companies I had posed in commercial advertising. But they were all more than twice my age, and I thought this a poor basis for a sustained relationship. I also knew that when wealthy businessmen contracted with a model for commercial advertising, they had a tendency to assume payment was not only for camera time and product endorsement but also represented an advance for personal face and body time as well. They could as easily think of marriage as something like leasing a wife, and when interest waned, opt out and rent a new one.

Men would follow me all the time, but I feared sex and pregnancy, so no one could tease even one kiss from me. I loved no one, and I, who had once dreamed of marrying someone special, wearing a white bridal gown, now only thought of how to care for my daughter and assure her health.

Exasperated, unhappy in a bodyguard role, Father eventually introduced me to one of his younger neighborhood friends, an air force technician who had musical interest and even creative ability, as proven by his having written a few songs. Thus, in October 1958, not yet twenty, pushed by my family, I married Phung Nam Luong (composer Hoai Nam) and, just as my father and mother had thought, taking that step did provide some insulation from improper assumptions and advances. Although I was not enveloped by the special warmth of love that I always dreamed would be basic to marriage, we two did have a shared interest in music. In the beginning, Luong would occasionally bring some of his friends to hear me sing, and we sometimes talked about which songs were most suitable for my voice. Our first son, Phung Quoc Bao ("national protector"), was born the following year in July 1959.

But while I supposed my personal life was entering a period of apparent stability, the same could not be said of my country. Communist-led unrest became a painful characteristic of life in the hamlets, especially in provinces where the Viet Minh had been ascendant, if not dominant, during the war for independence. Our government had foregone what in 1955 and 1956, and perhaps even 1957, was an opportunity for generating citizen inclusion to develop rural southern loyalty supporting a noncommunist future.

Looking back, more than sixty years past, it is obvious that by 1959, our policies and inconsistent rural operations versus (by that time) increasing communist organization of opposition to the Republic of Viet Nam governance had brought both sides to the point where there would be renewed internal warfare. That very year, our government issued a new decree establishing mobile field courts with the power to immediately judge, and even order the execution of, suspected wrongdoers on the spot. It seemed to me that what I was told about those courts was a resurrection of former French colonial practice, and I thought Vietnamese should not conduct themselves against other Vietnamese that way. But I was just twenty years old, a dancer and singer of songs. I had many questions, but I doubted anyone of influence was interested in my opinion. And I had a new ongoing personal problem.

My husband was not simply an acquaintance of my father. They were occasional alcoholic drinking companions, and the frequency and amount consumed did not decrease for either of them. Luong would too often come home at odd hours, stumble into the bedroom and, by hurried demonstration of need, expect me to be instantly available for "on demand" physical demonstration of love. Roused from sleep. I was expected to comply, but it was not easy. I was always tired. My singing is, in a real sense, the expression of who I am, but performing was also financially necessary, not just for Luong, Bao, Le Thu, and me, but also for my parents, who were accustomed to receiving frequent sums.

Furthermore, besides the time required for travel to venues and performing, I was still expected to keep our home clean, prepare meals as needed, and care for Bao when not away from the house. I was exhausted! Luong, numbed by alcohol, never understood the pressure that I felt. He would always expect to have his way. Over time, complaints and insistence became a platform for abuse. Marital circumstances, in and out of bed, were increasingly unhappy for both of us, but most painful for me.

Beyond our own family, the republic established and led by President Diem and his family was increasingly at risk. In January 1960, there was a larger than usual attack against government forces in the Tay Ninh Province, less than a day's drive from Saigon. Our nerves were shaken, but overall tension was not the only consequence of a threat posed by a revived, very aggressive communist military. Lack of real representation within the government for all kinds of non-communists meant that participation in decision-making and implementing policy was limited to one family and the few personalities among their chorus. I began to hear complaints from politically interested persons in Saigon. Many of them were friends who wrote newspaper or magazine columns by day, like Nguyen Trong Chat (pen name Trong Minh), and who would frequent one or more entertainment venues by night.

In April 1960, a group of former senior officials and out-of-favor political and religious leaders held a meeting in the Caravelle Hotel and prepared a petition to the president asking for administrative and political reform. The official response was more than just negative; the government became even more restrictive. And in our neighborhood, ordinary people began to speak softly about police abuse, including night raids to abduct persons who were thought to be government critics.

The new military, especially paratroop officers—who more than any other had strongly supported the president in 1955—now five years later began to fracture. Some whom my family knew personally, like Do Cao Tri[2] and his young brother Do Cao Luan, were still strongly committed to the president, believing, as I sometimes heard them say, that there was no realistic alternative. Others, and they seemed increasing in number, were beginning to speak about the need for change at the top and reform of appointments to command. I was always careful to listen, even while refraining from expressing my own opinion. I had great respect for the president, but the case for change that was being whispered in cabarets and coffee shops was persistent and persuasive.

In November, an influential group of those young officers, unsurprisingly led by paratroopers, and chiefly Nguyen Chanh Thi,[3] put together a sort of coup attempt that began by surrounding the presidential residence and offices, but thereafter stalled due to lack of a comprehensive plan. I knew two of them, from their occasional appearances at musical events organized to support morale. They were good men, and they did not seem to be grasping for personal power. They appeared, instead, by almost polite request, intent on obtaining military and political reforms. Their sincerity was proven by their lack of decisive aggressive movement against the presidential palace. At the beginning, when they could have assaulted and seized the surrounding presidential grounds, they behaved instead as if it were sufficient to appear with requests, as petitioners might have done in earlier times when seeking an audience with the emperor.

Relatively senior officers, the generals who were previously French lackeys and beneficiaries of colonial privilege, paused to evaluate

---

[2] Do Cao Tri was born into a relatively wealthy family of Bien Hoa Province in 1929. My father's family, also southern, was acquainted with some of the Do family. Do Cao Tri commanded the airborne battalions from 1954 to 1955 and was an important figure in defeating the Binh Xuyen forces. He was key to the 1963 toppling of the First Republic, but by 1965 his disagreement with General Nguyen Khanh brought about his exile until his return to important army commands before his death in a February 1971 helicopter crash near the Cambodia and Tay Ninh border.

[3] Nguyen Chanh Thi was born in Hue in 1923. He commanded the airborne units involved in the 1960 reformist demonstration/quasi-coup. An object of jealousy and suspicion from other generals, he was exiled in 1966 and died in Pennsylvania in 2007.

their own prospects. While the president equivocated, tempting petitioners to hope that he might be responsive to the need for change, and as the paratroopers and their allies milled about, the older self-interested generals arrived late to the party with reinforcements to support the president and the status quo that was best for themselves. Paratrooper and marine leaders, sensing the scales tipping against them, withdrew to the Tan Son Nhut airfield and availed themselves of a C-47 to make an escape to exile in Cambodia. Rather than understanding the event as signaling a need for reform, our president and his family implemented increasingly repressive policies thereafter.

I was intimately familiar with that syndrome, because in my own personal life whenever I asked Luong to consider my feelings and be more supportive of my trying to be homemaker, mother, wife, and the person who earned most of the family income, his response would usually be a promise to be more understanding and a true partner, followed very soon by resumption of alcohol-fueled verbal and physical abuse. He was insistent that everything—any issue or problem—be understood as he defined it, even though his way was not easily explainable. He had once been happy with my growing reputation as a popular singer and brought his friends to listen; but now there was resentment for the applause and attention accorded me.

Men, foreign as well as Vietnamese, often gazed upon me in cabarets and later followed me from venue to venue, imagining they were somehow making special contact. Among the most persistent, and therefore worst from my perspective, was an officer of the Philippine embassy, an attaché colonel, who would sometimes press envelopes with money upon my driver. Once, he even followed my family to Vung Tau and, in an effort to force me into conversation, removed spark plugs from my car after I had left it parked while shopping. On that occasion I beat him with a bamboo stave grabbed from a street vendor and asked the Vietnamese police to order him away from my family.

Luong never understood. I was not provoking men; I was being imposed upon. He was changing into an ever more jealous tyrant. It was not enough for him to control me at home. Now he wanted other men to see him exercise control, domination, in public. He would unpredictably appear at any cabaret, any evening, and when his drunken rage erupted, patrons would move far away, some even departing. Most restaurant owners, aggravated by the impact on their business, would blame me and require that Luong leave. I would be embarrassed, he would drink even more, and the following hours at home would be a nightmare.

Despite this increasingly desperate situation, like many women in similar circumstances, I was inclined by our culture to believe that it was my responsibility to accept the situation and do all that I could to maintain the marriage. Any sentimental regard diminished, but responding to the societal imperative and Luong's expectations, I was once again pregnant the next year and my second son, Phung Quoc Khai ("national victor"), was born in December 1961.

Even today, sixty years later, I sometimes wonder if my problem was solely due to the culture of which I was part or whether difficulty with an abusive husband was replicating a pattern seen between my mother and father. I tried not to think about that because I knew my mother was often miserable when father went in search of another woman or took family money to drink and gamble, later returning home angry. My father was an unrestrained philanderer, and soon the family-expense money that derived from my earnings, or at least the portion he could wrest away from mother, was not sufficient for him. Father owned a small print shop, was technically competent, and was personable when sober. But he borrowed against the shop to fuel his irresponsible lifestyle, and when unable to repay that debt, the small but profitable printing enterprise was forfeit.

Even as I tried to comfort Mother when her life was most unhappy, my own was simultaneously no better. Luong was so demanding of my acquiescence and obedience to his every whim that sometimes he would hold me by the throat and shake me with such violence that when finally released, I could not stand. From time to time, he would tell me that I should abandon singing. It just did not register with him that his own income was not enough to support our family of three children while still assisting my parents as I had been doing since before marriage. He used threats against our two sons as leverage to force compliance. If I were not sufficiently responsive, he would twist one of the boys by the arm or ear until they would cry out for me. Once he had the youngest, Khai, spread his arms and kneel for most of the day even though the child was barely more than a year old. On another occasion, when I returned home and heard Khai crying, Luong refused to respond to my knocking on the door. I had to climb on our neighbor's roof to enter a second-floor window, gain entry, and comfort my son.

The physical abuse and emotional stress month after month were undiminished. My best friend during that time was Tran Thi Hoa. She accompanied me to all the clubs and restaurants where I sang, usually three songs at each, and she witnessed my smile while performing, a smile that masked the hurt within. Once while moving by taxi to the next event, she suddenly began to cry. When I asked why, she said it was for me that her tears flowed. I have always remembered her sympathy and good heart.

Whenever I would appear at a club with a bruised face or marks on my throat, other friendly singers would sometimes cry for me. Of course, as you may have already supposed, I would steadfastly lie by saying that I had accidentally hurt myself while cleaning the house or fallen while playing with my children. No one taught me those evasions of truth; it seems to be our transcultural and millennia-practiced woman's response. I did not ask anyone whether there could be a solution or what would be best for me to do. The notions of family therapy, even treatment for alcoholism, were unknown in the Saigon of those years. I only understood, at last and with pain, that I had to somehow save myself and my three children.

My emotional and mental trauma were severe. Even years later, after legal separation and eventual divorce, I still felt a residual misery due to having so long suffered abuse. I believe that women around the world, if they emerge from a cruel marriage, either character- ized by socially sanctioned male psychosis or perhaps a substance dependency–fueled distortion of the male role within family, will understand the persistence of those wounds. When strangers asked years later about the father of Khai and Bao, I fabricated an alternate history, mentioning casually that he had been in the military and died when his plane crashed. A lie seemed preferable to the painful truth of having tolerated mistreatment of myself and my children.

The most influential woman in southern Viet Nam at that time was Tran Le Xuan, wife of Ngo Dinh Nhu, sister-in-law of President Diem, leader of the Women's Solidarity Movement, a flame-throwing activist, as people might say today. In 1958, she forced passage of legislation codifying family law that made divorce extremely difficult, almost impossible. Ostensibly for the protection of women, and perhaps true for most, it bound me within a psycho- logically and physically abusive marriage.

Rising tension in Saigon prompted me to make a decision that would change all our lives. Two Viet Nam Air Force pilots, flying American attack aircrafts, bombed President Diem's official residence and presidential offices one morning in February 1962. Opposition to the rule of the Ngo family had transitioned from coffee house and cabaret whining to political petition, then a well-intentioned but failed semi-coup, and now this blatant attempt to kill the president and any of his family who might have been within bomb-blast range.

I thought Saigon might soon resemble the conflicted city it had been in 1945 when my parents and I had escaped to Tra Vinh. But now where should we go? I knew there was a new general policy to convert every rural hamlet into a small, fenced community, Ap Chien Luoc (strategic hamlet), for self-defense against communist attacks. Remembering my grandparents' idyllic life, with homes along canals and smaller waterways and noble old shade trees, I foresaw that compressing and fencing rural communities would inconvenience too many families south of Saigon. That dislocation would fuel discontent, which in turn would be exploitable by the communist political cadre, the same sort of men who motivated my people to resist the French in 1945. So reasoning, I ruled out any consideration of returning to the Mekong province that I knew as a child because it would have meant moving to an area where communists were already growing in strength.

Later that year, Tran Le Xuan, increasingly influential, forced through the rubber-stamp National Assembly a new package of laws setting standards of public morality. Per those laws, dancing, among other defined immoral behaviors, was outlawed. Of course, there was an instant impact on every nightclub and restaurant owner. Their business activity abruptly declined. Correspondingly, my income based on singing in those same venues withered.

I dillydallied for a few months. Maybe, we thought, the new general situation might not be so bad, so permanent, as we feared. But in January 1963, there was a sharp two-day battle between communist units and Republic of Viet Nam forces using tanks and helicopters near My Tho, only about forty miles southwest of Saigon, just an hour or so from where we lived. Newspapers and radio all reported a government victory at Ap Bac, but the scale of that engagement so close to the capital was alarming.

I convinced my parents that we had to move to a safer area right away. And there was an immediate, and interesting, opportunity to relocate to Dalat, a sort of hill station resort that had never been a communist target. Dalat was a six-hour drive northeast of Saigon and had a healthy climate that would be beneficial for my children, especially Le Thu. I had already separated from Luong, taking my children to stay with Mother and Father and making the change of relationship legal with the assistance of a lawyer. Now moving far from Saigon would solve two problems: I would not suffer daily threats of spousal aggression, and we would be safe from political intrigue and the increasing insurgent activity in and around Saigon. In February 1963, two or three weeks after Tet, the Lunar New Year, we leaped away to Dalat and a new life.

The Dalat option was premised on renting a three-story shop on Minh Mang Street, downhill from the main market. Mother had saved enough of my money, hiding it from Father, to allow us to make a deposit and advance a few months' rental. We would operate a coffee shop on the ground floor and the one above, and our family could temporarily live, crowded, in the space on the third floor. In the beginning we had to renovate the premises. I wanted our coffee shop to be a place that would have a sophisticated appearance but obviously open for welcoming everyone, not just moneyed Dalat residents and visitors. Another good friend, Ton Thi Kim Chi, who occasionally sang in clubs, accompanied us. I was thankful to have her with me. Everyone worked hard, even my father, to clean up, make alterations, and decorate. We installed interior bamboo trim, added artistic embellishment throughout, and put in beautiful plate-glass windows with a large sign proclaiming our coffee shop name: "KIVINI."

We were almost ready to open for customers when, without warning, a mini catastrophe fell upon us. Despite having warned Luong that his continual abuse was intolerable and that I was taking responsibility for the children, and even though we were at last legally separated, one day he sought us out in our Dalat sanctuary. Luong arrived in an alcohol-fueled rage and, while threatening me, broke the coffee shop windows bearing our business's name. I had to call the Dalat police. Luong was arrested and confined. I felt obligated, because of our shared past and his being the father of my two sons, to ask the police chief to guarantee that Luong would not be mistreated. However, I also wanted the police to forcefully warn him to stay away from Dalat in the future. We did have to replace those plate-glass windows, but the cost would be bearable if Luong would, at last, allow me my freedom.

CHAPTER 5

Love Found

D alat was absolute heaven for our family. It was not a tropical paradise—as someone unfamiliar with the geography of Viet Nam might suppose—because the mile-high elevation in the central highlands means that the daytime temperature is never hot. Evenings are cool, usually requiring a sweater or jacket. Tall leafy trees, different from any seen in Tra Vinh or Saigon, and fresh-smelling pine forests— rather than palms, banana trees, and other lowland flora—are typical. Swift-flowing streams and waterfalls are constant in every season. Flowers, among them orchids and roses, bloom year-round.

Small family farms surrounded Dalat, especially to the west. Nearby small hill towns, at a slightly lower altitude, had markets with produce from vegetable farms in their respective areas. Rich soil combined with intensive cultivation by the farming families resulted in such abundance, especially of cabbage and cauliflower, that produce was sent to Saigon by road every day. Our own Dalat market was so overflowing that what was not sold fresh would be deeply discounted the next day. Some families just beyond the city terraced hillsides to cultivate coffee and tea, while others specialized in farming fruit. I remember that Dalat strawberry wine became a favorite because it was sweet rather than simply intoxicating.

The town itself had been nicely laid out by our previous colonial rulers, with generally broad streets throughout residential areas, even in the market neighborhood. An artificial lake, Ho Xuan Huong, achieved by damming a small stream, was on the northern edge of Dalat and was often sought out by residents for slow walks as they conversed about the pleasures of life in a part of Viet Nam untouched by war. The climate meant that most Vietnamese were unusually fair skinned, and the Dalat girls could bat their eyes flirtatiously above healthy pink cheeks.

There were some resident foreigners: residual French lingering as medical practitioners, professors in Catholic schools, and proprietors of restaurants. Vietnamese were most numerous in the town and on small farm, but tribespeople (I believe mostly Koho and Churu) brought their handicrafts and forest products to the Dalat market for sale. We would see them, dressed in home-woven dark blue or even darker, almost black, clothing with embroidered borders, in and around the market stalls. I never sensed any hostility among the locals. The remnant French, whether affiliated with boarding schools, religious missions, or modest medical offices, appeared simply reluctant to leave a country they had come to think of as more home than where they were born.

There were only a few Americans, and most of those were advisors with the National Military Academy on the north side of Dalat. The younger ones often came to our coffee shop in the evenings, and one or two would direct a lingering gaze in my direction. But I was a child no longer and could discern any problematic intent. So, while I may have appeared alluring, I was simultaneously not easily approachable, especially since I could always retreat behind the cashier's counter.

A young American agricultural specialist named Dan occasionally appeared in the evening. He worked with the chief of provincial agricultural services, a man with two captivating daughters. The eldest, Uyen Nhu, had been engaged to one of the pilots who the previous year bombed the presidency. She was arrested, jailed, and brutally interrogated for several months. Most people in Dalat, cautious and fearing contamination by association, avoided her family. I thought most people mean.

The most interesting American, because I harbored a secret intention to learn some English, was named Douglas Ramsey. He was a frequent evening visitor to the coffee shop, always well mannered, and an avid speaker of Vietnamese with almost every one of our customers. That really impressed me because I had never before heard a foreigner expressing thoughts in our language, conversing so fluently, with no strained pause to string words together. Listening with closed eyes, one would think he must be Vietnamese. I thought that since I already spoke some French, another foreign language could not be too difficult. Douglas had an office, a branch of the USIS, in a small building where he supervised English teaching and occasionally showed an evening film. It was in the "government" section of Dalat, across the street (more or less) from an Air Viet Nam ticketing office, not far from the provincial headquarters, and downhill from the Dalat Palace Hotel. I thought to wait for an opportune moment to enquire about classes.

Although Luong was now far away, the disturbing episode of his intrusion convinced me that we should change our living arrangements. If our family could always be easily found by checking first at the coffee shop, where of course for business reasons I would necessarily spend much time welcoming guests, then repeated intrusions on our personal life would be difficult to avoid. The best way to resolve that problem would be to rent a house. Our family would be more comfortable, and it would be easier to ensure privacy than when living upstairs in our place of business.

We found a house that was available. It was old and needed restoration, but it did have electricity and running (but cold) water. It needed a lot of work. We could do that over time, but I hated the idea of making improvements to property that, in the end, would still belong to someone else. When I hesitantly expressed that opinion to the owner, who lived with his family in a house next door, he responded that the property could be purchased as easily as rented. As easily as rented! As though I had that much money! But we talked and bargained, and talked and bargained, until I asked for time to attempt arrangements. Mother and I went to Saigon and sold all our accumulated family jewelry. By scrambling and scraping here and there, we were able to collect what was necessary to purchase our Dalat home.

The villa, probably once owned by members of the colonial middle-class French, was stucco with tile roofing, featured a front reception area and dining room at the center, and had two bedrooms at each end of the main house. A smaller separate kitchen structure with three small bedrooms for staff was just a few steps from the rear back door and was arrived at beneath a covered walkway. Although necessary immediate repairs were required, then eventual updating and improvements, I loved the place and right away began to plan how to best fix the two connected buildings. And from the very first day I dreamed of arranging a floral garden and installing a small fishpond within the spacious front yard.

Ton Thi Kim Chi, of all my friends the closest, had accompanied our family from Saigon and helped to organize the coffee shop. Now she acted there in my place while I focused on making the new (for us) house ready for everyone. Kim Chi always encouraged me, and above all, her cheerful companionship while I organized my life, settling parents and three children, was indispensable. When I reflect on my life, I feel blessed to have had such a good and understanding woman my own age for a companion and constant friend.

Another sort of pilgrim in our party was an uncle who drove the old Citroën auto that I purchased with earnings from my singing engagements. He was unflinchingly cheerful, even while loading and unloading for the move from Saigon to Dalat and now from the coffee shop apartment to the house. We were all busy, but content, in those early months. Even Father seemed to have changed. Perhaps that was because we were six or seven hours from Saigon and temptation. His behavior seemed moderated by our new life in Dalat—or was I just perceiving what I had always wanted to see?

Two young Viet Nam Army instructors at the Dalat Military Academy introduced me to horseback riding. Lieutenants Toan and Khue very respectfully made sure I would always ride in a safe area along the lake. I was literally a raw beginner and did not sit on a horse as skillfully as my friends. I had an accident, no fault of the horse, that landed me unconscious in the Soulier Clinic. Upon waking, I was astonished to see by my bed that same Philippine colonel who I had thought permanently discouraged of any notion that he might in some way keep me company. Learning of my hospitalization from a Saigon friend, he immediately drove six hours from Saigon to Dalat, thinking there might be a bedside opportunity to persuasively express his fervent sentiments. He was envious and frustrated to find me already surrounded by several young Vietnamese officers from the military academy, two of whom felt some special guilt for having arranged the horse that threw me. My alarm was soothed by their presence retarding the colonel's ardor, and I was even more greatly relieved when informed by Kim Chi a day later that the unwelcome visitor had returned to Saigon.

For the first time since I had been a child myself, now by bringing Le Thu, Bao, and Khai to the waterfalls near Dalat—especially Prenn, where there was a rudimentary zoo—or splashing in the slower Cam Ly stream near the seldom-used military airfield, enjoying picnics by Xuan Huong Lake, and strolling in and out of shops around the Dalat market, I experienced through my children a mind-opening appreciation for how grand, how consciousness-expanding, life ought to be. We four, sometimes with Kim Chi, would be out and among people daily, but unlike in Saigon, here in Dalat no one bothered me. I resumed occasionally riding horses on the rolling hills north of the lake. Time passed in a smooth, soothing rhythm.

I learned to ride in Dalat and continued to do so as a distraction from personal difficulty.

All seemed well, in circumstances altogether better for me and my family in Dalat, and I even hoped there might be some slow improvement in Saigon and the provinces that would yield fair, popular government. But in early May, only a few days before my twenty-fourth birthday, there was a police confrontation with Buddhists on the streets of Hue, our stately former capital. The secretive Can Lao party chapter at the military academy in Dalat provided commandant and staff with the official version of what had happened. My two instructor friends shared that information, leavened by their personal skepticism, with me. Another friend, a singer like me who had been visiting friends in Hue, paused for a weekend rest in Dalat en route back to Saigon. Her perspective was significantly different from the Can Lao party account.

Just before a traditional celebration of Buddha's birthday, she told me, the Hue municipal administration reconfirmed a ban on displaying religious flags, even though days earlier Vatican flags were allowed to be flown to celebrate the president's brother, Archbishop Ngo Dinh Thuc. When a large number of Buddhist flags appeared on the streets in Hue, Archbishop Thuc saw them as a personal affront. He complained to the city government and to presidential brother Ngo Dinh Can who, a resident in Hue, was the virtual ruler on behalf of the Ngo family. Police forces suppressed a Buddhist demonstration the next day, and because several people were killed, the issue quickly became a rallying cause for Buddhists while fracturing the national government consensus. My personal reaction as a Catholic was tempered by having many Buddhist friends and a supposition that while there could have been communist agitators in monk robes, there were surely Catholic communists, too.

I held my own counsel, lest someone report me as anti-government, but I thought that President Diem could restore government credibility only if a prompt personal apology and remedial action were initiated by himself, not delegated. Many of us wondered why he did not do what should have been logical. More than fifty years later I still believe the president could have applied correctives. Why did he fail to do so? I think it was because the problem was created by his brother Archbishop Thuc, and further snarled by their younger brother Can, who exercised authority in that region on behalf of the family. President Diem was unable to undercut his brothers, even though he should have done just that.

Rumors of political tension, government paralysis, and continuing consequences of Buddhist-Catholic tensions, drifted our way from Saigon during the summer months, but we in Dalat only wished for the grim news to ebb away from our mountaintop.

My children were attending a good school, and I though it timely for me to enquire about learning English. The next time Douglas Ramsey came for coffee, and before he could begin roaming tables to strike up conversations in Vietnamese with other customers, I quickly sat down opposite him and blurted out that I wanted to learn English, and although I supposed he did not actually teach all the classes, I would appreciate his special help to place me in the right section with a very good teacher who could also speak some Vietnamese.

I was about to be disappointed, because he responded, although in a most considerate manner, that the best way to really learn English would be with someone who could not speak Vietnamese at all, because then I would have to concentrate and study even harder than if I were with a teacher who could speak my own language. Moreover, Douglas continued, he was about to leave Dalat. He would transfer to Qui Nhon in Central Viet Nam, and another American would come from that town to replace him in Dalat. I asked whether the new director would teach English. Douglas smiled, even laughed just a bit, and replied that he rather doubted so, but he promised to introduce me to the new person so I could enquire myself.

A couple of weeks passed, and Douglas Ramsey was absent—no more coffee shop visits. Then one evening, after coming downstairs from the second floor that was usually frequented by officials and moneyed business owners, I saw him sitting with another foreigner whose back was to me. I hurried over to remind Douglas of his promise to introduce me to the new and helpful (I hoped) English teaching director. I was in such a hurry I stumbled and steadied myself by clutching their table.

"Are you here for long? And when will the new director be coming?" I asked anxiously, embarrassed by my clumsiness. "Well," he responded, "here he is, and his name is Frank." I turned to look at the man whose back had been to me before I careened past in my eagerness to query Doug.

I cannot describe the impact of looking into those eyes: gray, light blue, green—a mix of all those colors. He smiled, lightly, and

Douglas Ramsey with me and Frank, 1963.

I suddenly felt unexpectedly off-balance. I stayed standing by the table, feeling as though I were a feather: inconsequential, weak, unable to move and speechless. It was my occasional nightmare that I would appear before an audience to sing and be unable to make a sound. Now I really was just so, struck mute, right in my own coffee shop and for no good reason at all.

Faithful reader, if you have come with me this far, I do not know whether you will agree or understand even if you disagree with the following: I think that we may, unconsciously, carry within ourselves, somewhere deep, an image, a shadow, a sort of vague profile—like an old-fashioned photo negative—of the person with whom we anticipate sharing life. Now suddenly, with no warning, here he was, right there, right before me. I had never felt even slightly that way before. I was still gripping the table when Douglas Ramsey asked if I might have hurt myself. I assured them both that I was fine. But I was not fine at all.

I felt as though turned upside down, head spinning, experiencing vertigo. I do not even remember how I walked back to converse with Kim Chi beside the cash register. That night I asked myself over and over, "*Troi oi* (God above), what happened?" The man was a foreigner! I must have mistaken my own reaction. I tripped and had almost fallen; I had been dizzy, faint, but not because of him. It could not be. Sleep came slowly that night. I felt perturbed, even irritable, for my own foolish reaction. I told myself that when I saw him again it would be with no special feeling. In fact, I could not even remember his name. He would only be another coffee-sipping customer. And, as I thought further, there really was no need for me to study English.

The next day, Kim Chi asked whether I was feeling poorly. She said that I looked feverish, as though I had not slept well, and she asked whether it might have to do with the young American who had been with Douglas.

"Not at all," I replied. "You will see for yourself when he comes today. He is only another customer."

But that new customer didn't come back for several days. Entirely all right with me! When he finally reappeared in our coffee shop, Kim Chi was at the cash register. She called me on the upstairs phone, interrupting my conversation with important guests, and reported that a certain special American had returned. I took my time, meaning that I checked my appearance in the mirror, and only then raced down the stairs. But I halted before entering the first-floor public area, catching my breath and adopting a cool and indifferent pose.

He sat at the cashier's bar, talking with Kim Chi. He smiled when looking in my direction. Kim Chi murmured, but distinctly, that I had missed him. "Not so," I insisted, "but we are a coffee shop and need every customer." He smiled again, eyes warm and friendly, but almost paralyzing me at the same time, and told us that when in Dalat, coming to KIVINI would be his regular habit. He was speaking Vietnamese with us, not as correctly as Douglas Ramsey always did, but with ease. He said that after recently spending a few days with Douglas around Qui Nhon and Quang Ngai, he would now be in Dalat for a week or so.

I advised him that important customers—generals, colonels, officials, and businesspeople—always took their coffee on the second floor, and he could join them when coming to our shop. But he replied that the first floor, right at street level, suited him perfectly. The mix of soldiers, students, and others, he said, would probably be more interesting than what could be found on the second floor.

During the next several days he usually came in the evening, took his coffee in the public area, and ventured above only once, as though curious as to what fauna might be found at a higher elevation. One evening, just at closing, I asked whether he could drive me around Dalat in his jeep to take some fresh air before I joined Kim Chi for cleanup. For a moment he hesitated, looking almost embarrassed, then agreed. We drove on the quiet residential streets and around Xuan Huong Lake, slowly, and I did relish the cool mountain atmosphere. While bringing me back to KIVINI, he said it would be another week or two before he would be returning for coffee. He needed to spend time in other provinces but hoped to have an evening drive with me again. I only nodded and thanked him, but his hope was mine too.

So, he had really come once more, bewildered me, and then, as quickly as he came, went away. But I had much more to do than simply pine for him. Le Thu was seven years old and in classes at Le Couvent des Oiseaux. Her health was much improved after frequent hospitalizations and medical treatments in Saigon, but now during a period of growth, her spinal column irregularity reappeared, requiring frequent appointments at the Soulier Clinic in Dalat. My two sons, Bao and Khai, were occasionally mischievous, doing well in school at the French *petit lycée* but needing my steady attention to monitor and correct their behavior.

My mother was indispensably supportive, helping with physical therapy for Le Thu and watching the boys while I worked at the coffee shop. My dear friend Kim Chi continued to oblige as the reliable resourceful cashier and manager for our coffee shop. The sole difficulty for both of us was that my father was itching to get his hands into the till, so he would grasp any opportunity to criticize Kim Chi and injure the relationship between her and me.

Late in October, well into the highlands dry season and with mountain evenings cooling, Frank was back in our Dalat coffee shop again. He said, with a mesmerizing smile, that he had been traveling in Central Viet Nam, then to Saigon, and had returned to see me. He came back to see me! I didn't care where he had been; my heart was simply gripped by the notion that he may have returned, after all my own confusion of feelings, thinking of me as I had been thinking of him. That same night we again drove through the Dalat streets, past the market uphill from my shop, and around part of the lake. Frank took me past a large house on Tran Hung Dao Street and, as we passed, said that was where he stayed when in Dalat. I thought he might ask whether I would like to see the inside, but we were quickly past the driveway and still moving away. I was relieved, not knowing how I might have responded. I dreamed of him, yes, but despite the heartfelt emotional, electric charge . . . we still barely knew each other.

But he did reach for my hand, and sensing that he wanted to touch, I responded and clasped his hand as he held mine. There was an instantaneous special feeling—not really of desire at this first intimate gesture, but his hand felt warm, and not only in contrast to the cool wind passing through the canvas-covered jeep. The sensation touched more than my hand. I swear it coursed through me, and I clasped his hand tightly, hoping that he would understand that something important, more than physicality, was connecting us. I felt sheltered, protected. Whenever he withdrew his hand to shift the gears, I would move my own slightly closer to ease reconnection. Too soon, I thought, we were at my door. Acknowledging the change from acquaintanceship to something more had been achieved by the fleeting embrace of hands. As soon as I entered the building, with my hand still warm and tingling, Kim Chi said, smiling, that it looked as though I were falling in love. I told her that she should know better. I was far past falling over anyone.

Even so, I was disappointed when, on the next evening, Frank stopped in the coffee shop only briefly, barely sitting a few moments with Kim Chi and me. He said there was much that needed doing at his house, including preparing for visitors. I understood that his address was more workplace than home, and I did appreciate his coming to let me know that we could not repeat our evening drive. At the same time, it troubled me to think he considered a potential visitor more significant than the little time we could share.

The following day, late in the afternoon, the police official who previously assisted when my estranged husband Luong had threatened me came to our coffee shop to notify my father that on the next day there would be increased security on the streets because of important Saigon visitors. We wasted no time wondering who that might be, thinking only of the inconvenience to ourselves. Frank did not come to KIVINI that night. I never guessed he could have any connection to what was happening, caring only about his absence and not the reason why.

We learned only after their departure that President Diem and American Ambassador Lodge had been the important visitors to our mountain town. They arrived at the Cam Ly airfield, stayed one night, and returned immediately to Saigon. Knowing they met in Dalat provided me with some personal relief, and for two reasons. First, I understood that Frank really did have a good cause for not being with me the previous evening. Second, and less selfishly, I understood President Diem was caught in a delicate and dangerous political situation, partly caused by his own family. Making corrective adjustments would be difficult. Learning that the American ambassador traveled with President Diem, and that they met for discussion in Dalat, caused me to hope that Americans were helping Vietnamese peacefully resolve a volatile situation.

When Frank came by the coffee shop late that evening, he casually mentioned that his part of the visit had been to meet Ambassador Lodge and his wife at the airfield, wait with them until President Diem landed in a separate plane, and then bring the ambassador to his house for conversation before escorting them to the presidential guest house. Frank spent the night alone in his home in case the ambassador might have some need for him, but they did not reconnect. I asked whether he knew anything about the discussion between President Diem and Ambassador Lodge. He responded that he had not attended that meeting and so could not know much about their conversation.

I leaned back in my chair, wondering how my country's relationship with America could be so important and still such a puzzle. Despite not learning anything from Frank, I believed it encouraging that the American ambassador had met with President Diem in Dalat, far from the intrigues of Saigon. And, more significant from a purely personal perspective, when Frank and I resumed our late-evening drives about town, it was always with clasped hands.

Only three days later, on November 1, President Diem was overthrown and murdered by a traitorous band of generals. These were the same men the president had promoted and trusted to protect the Republic of Viet Nam. Knowing that Ambassador Lodge just had a private conversation with the president in Dalat, I could not understand why the Americans had not used their influence to arrive at a political solution, rather than standing mutely aside or perhaps even encouraging a murderous change of government that avoided any constitutional pretense. I knew some of those generals and colonels who seized power, and whatever their rationale, I doubted not only their motives but also their ability to govern.

And now, right after that catastrophe, Frank was gone again. He was customarily vague about where he would travel, what he might be doing, and whom he would be working with, but this time, he casually mentioned driving to Saigon for a meeting with his supervisor and friends. He would be absent only a few days, but knowing he drove on roads that many others would not choose, I began to pray for him every night. Despite a typically Vietnamese approach to daily life—a sort of Buddhist-Catholic methodology—and not entirely persuaded of the power of prayer, I was at least sure that supplication for a loved one could not hurt, and might, even if it were only a "maybe," help the one whose image was in my heart.

After Frank returned from Saigon, we had a more than a casual political discussion for the first time. He told me that during the days and nights of his living and traveling within hamlets of other provinces before coming to Dalat, he had seen repeated Viet Nam government errors that aggravated problems instead of solving them. He believed the two most significant were a lack of respect from appointed officials for the citizens, especially those living in the countryside, and casual unthinking measures that worsened tension between Buddhists and Catholics. Unfortunately, he thought, the change of government so far did not indicate that the collection of military officers newly in control would do any better; he concluded that they might well be worse.

Well, I asked, would not the American embassy provide good counsel, advisory guidance, for the right path? He shook his head slowly, and replied that he did not feel anyone, maybe especially including Americans, had a workable plan based on placing the best people in the right positions for defining goals, with concepts and principles for objectively measuring progress.

He told me that he would once more leave in a day or two for travel in provinces to the north. I suggested the possibility of my accompanying him, but with a wry smile he responded that would not be possible. I knew very well that his interest in Dalat was limited to me, but my heart ached a bit and felt a need to know more. He often played with my children and was friendly with my parents and grandfather. They of course were beginning to wonder about the extent of my relationship with Frank. It was easy for others to speculate but difficult for me because I never knew for sure where he was and what he was doing. I really knew too little about him.

Frustrated, I decided to go to Saigon for a few days while Frank was away from Dalat. I found that friends in the capital, many of them entertainers like myself, but also businesspeople, writers, and some artists, assumed that Americans had directed everything that happened in our country during recent months. I was not so sure. I thought instead that there were always deep, historic currents flowing within Viet Nam, and foreigners would forever be ignorant of what was below the surface, unaware of what Vietnamese were feeling and thinking.

At the same time, I also understood that the still recent colonial experience beneath the French boot inclined many to assume a foreign power could be more determinative than we Vietnamese in our own country. I had an impression that the new Saigon leaders—the generals and their friends—might really be more dependent on foreigners than the previous government of President Diem, and that would almost guarantee that they would stumble while considering governing policies.

Now it was apparent that, compared to one or two years earlier, there were many more Americans in Saigon. We saw them everywhere. Vietnamese, at least in our small cities and towns, had a generally favorable impression of Americans. We noted their informality, curiosity, and apparent sincerity. Still, after conversing with my friends, I wondered whether these friendly Americans might be too involved. It was not at all clear what role they played behind the scenes before and during the coup that disposed of the president and the constitutional government. Could we maintain our dignity and national identity while in harness with these friends? And could we prevail in a struggle against the new Viet Minh, a so-called South Viet Nam Liberation Front? Would Americans understand us, and would they be steadfast?

The violent change of government was brought to pass by ambitious generals and colonels, some of whom I had previously encountered while a popular singer. As soon as I returned to Dalat, it was obvious that they, self-centered as well as self-elevated, had more interest in celebrating themselves than focusing on necessary administrative affairs, both civil and military. Intoxicated with power that could only have been dreamed of previously, the new leaders reveled in promoting themselves and their friends to a higher grade. Colonels were propelled by opportunistic alliance to general, and generals grasped additional stars for adornment and as symbols of accomplishment, no matter how spurious. In November and December 1963, many of them made Dalat their playground, taking former imperial and presidential residences as the piratical prize and emblem of their newly acquired privilege. My family had to cater to them in our coffee shop. Sometimes we even had to smile and acquiesce when they so obviously expected that our gratitude for their presence should include complimentary beverages. Of course, they could have easily paid, but the supposition that we were honored by their presence was, for themselves, another proof of their new status. It is painful to recall, but that assumption of privilege and rude behavior was reminiscent of the characteristic Binh Xuyen gangster behavior.

I was invited, along with some entertainers and a few important Dalat officials, to a dinner party held in the former Bao Dai imperial residence by a few of the newly empowered generals. One of those generals, known to be an undisciplined womanizer, born in France and speaking that language better than he could Vietnamese, invited me to see the rooms above that were previously quarters for Bao Dai's wife, the empress before the royal family was deposed in 1955. He told me there was jade everywhere. I understood the risk in accepting but was curious to see the halls where former royals had traipsed. I was on guard, prepared to defend myself. And yes, when ascending the stairway toward the former royal chambers, Tran

Van Don grasped me and tried to steal a kiss while embracing me.[4] I quickly twisted away and pushed him so hard that he almost fell.

I told him, "You are a general of the army, and I am a simple singer, aren't you ashamed to trick me, to think you can force me to lie down with you?" Then as I moved rapidly away down that same stairway, I threatened to scream. He understood that not only were his equally opportunistic close friends attending the festive evening, there were too many other guests, potential witnesses, to risk an embarrassing scene. I went home immediately after.

When Frank returned to Dalat from his time spent in some of the central provinces, it seemed best not to tell him of my misadventure. I had protected myself, and I would be more cautious in the future. Frank needed to keep his attention focused on his own work, whatever that was. And, on the very first evening, driving around our romantic lake again, I learned that he would leave the next day, going to Saigon then onward to a southern province. He expected to be away for a few weeks.

My children and friends kept me busy, so there was no time for melancholy. Le Thu still required frequent medical checks, and Bao and Khai were as constantly active as any two little boys could be. Although Mother was a great help, my eyes and hands had to be ever present. Besides Kim Chi, my other good friends were the two young lieutenant-grade instructors at the Dalat Military Academy, Toan and Khue. Sometimes they took me to dances, and when we entered people would often glance in our direction and audibly murmur, "Mimosa . . . Mimosa." The mimosa of Dalat was a small shrub with pale flowers. I do not know, even to this day, why people associated me with mimosa.

---

[4] Tran Van Don (or "Andre," his French name) was born in France in 1917 and was first commissioned in the army of that country, later transferring to the Viet Nam army that was established by France. He was one of the key plotters of the seizure of power that resulted in the murder of President Diem in 1963 and the change of government to military rule. In and out of favor with other general officers, in 1975 he was briefly minister of defense before fleeing the country. Although he took residence in the United States, he died in France in 1998. He was cremated there, and his ashes remain in France.

One evening I met with an assembly of cadets. They gathered on the grass around me, politely asking for one or two songs, and enquiring about my family and what I supposed might be my future. They were so young, earnest in their curiosity, and sincere, that my heart was touched. I spoke with them too long, and therefore entirely because of me they were late returning to the academy and consequently disciplined the following day. No more informal assemblies and recitals!

Toan and Khue often visited our coffee shop and knew that I had special feelings for Frank. I think they both may have had a sort of worshipful love for me. There was safety for me in their keeping a cautious eye on each other. They always visited in tandem, and we would sometimes drive the children to a park or attend a film at the Dalat cinema near the market. I never favored one friend over the other, and they never presumed that there could be more than friendship. They definitely wondered what Frank might be doing when he was absent from Dalat, but since I did not know myself, their own curiosity would remain unsatisfied.

CHAPTER 6

LOVE EMBRACED

It was a few days after Christmas 1963, and Frank was back in Dalat. We spoke while he sipped coffee in our shop. He had just returned from observing conditions in Long An Province hamlets where, he told me, a young energetic Major Le Minh Dao was recently assigned as province chief.[5] Now, he believed, if Dao was a fair example of appointments by the new government, there might be real improvement in districts and provinces where the government would have a moral and vigorous administration. Fundamental to his thinking was that the most effective response to communist activity should be organizing small teams recruited, trained, and coordinated locally, but supported by the national government. The regular Viet Nam Army should be supplemental to local government and special teams rather than the reverse.

[5] Le Minh Dao was assigned as Long An Province chief in late 1963 following the overthrow and murder of President Diem, but he was removed after another change of government in 1964. Following staff assignments, he was made province chief in My Tho, where Frank met him again in 1969. As commanding general of the 18th Division, Le Minh Dao is justifiably best known for his battlefield courage and command presence in leading the defense of Xuan Loc against advancing communist forces in 1975. He survived years of captivity until his release to America, and died in March 2020.

I understood what he described because it was something like the civic action theory with which I was involved several years before, but I asked him how he could, as an American, be so sure. He responded that it ought to work because the practice was just tested and proven in Long An Province where he had recently spent days and nights in hamlets with local Vietnamese teams.

I had to interrupt, remembering my own experience and because I doubted whether any new government was prepared to operate very differently than before. So, I told him that decentralizing would mean sharing authority downward, and the generals were more likely to accumulate rather than disburse power. Frank replied that I may be right, but the situation just observed in Long An was so slippery that local action was required right away, and the national government would simply have to catch up. By "slippery," he explained, Long An Province, and other provinces as well, were slipping away into the hands of communist political organizers because of government inactivity and errors.

I agreed on that point. Recent conversation with friends in Saigon had already convinced me that the new military government was not sufficiently reorganizing ministries and offices for developing plans and programs that would serve the people and improve security. Everyone told me there was a sort of paralysis. I felt that our generals knew how to knock a government down but did not know how to build one up. This was a grim picture for me, but Frank, rather than appearing discouraged as I was, instead seemed to believe that in Long An there were new special-purpose teams that could prove to be a solution.

Once previously, I had dinner with him in the Dalat house on Tran Hung Dao Street. On that occasion we did no more than hold hands. I liked the woman, Chi Bay, who cooked for him and kept the house clean while he was gone. So now it seemed completely natural to accept another invitation, and Chi Bay greeted me as though we were sisters. While we were at the table, Frank explained that a new American officer, with his wife and son, would soon arrive in Dalat to manage the regular office work. Frank was already moving into the small guest quarters building adjacent to the main house so that the arriving family would have the larger home. Curious, I asked to see the guesthouse. It looked so small from the outside that I had thought it was meant only for storage. Now I wondered how the space within could be arranged for him. I assure you that I thought of nothing other than satisfying my curiosity.

We strolled across the graveled drive. Frank unlocked the entry to a little three-room sort of mountain cabin comprising a tiny kitchen and eating area, a small sitting room with a fireplace for cold Dalat nights, and a bedroom. Some of his clothing, a knapsack, guns of various sorts, and unrecognizable (at least by me) different pieces of equipment were strewn here and there. It was a mess, and I told him so! He placed his arms around me, promising to make the cottage neater, and said that he hoped I might still share dinner there with him from time to time. I lifted my face to assent. We were so close that a kiss, our first, was almost unavoidable and, anyway, eventually inevitable. So, the kiss, and then another, and another. In that small cottage we were within steps of the bedroom, then we were in that room and upon the bed.

What followed, despite my having had three children, was my first experience of total, unrestrained joyous intercourse. I had never felt that way before, and I could barely believe it was really me being so overwhelmed by a sensation of release and ecstasy. When I later returned home, it seemed as though I floated over the threshold and onward to my own room. I felt very different from the person I had been only a few hours earlier. Now I was sure that Frank was the man who would wrap me in the love I had dreamed of but lacked; a mutual commitment would guarantee our always being happy together.

Love is a complex composition. In a physical sense, many strands of neural circuits, subatomic particles—even pheromones, if you wish—combine metaphysically with imponderables, creating a sort of dream-walking reality. A glorious mystery compels exchanging independence for interdependency; care for each other includes shouldering the worry for the safety and well-being of the other, an added anxiety, and, of course, potential heartache. Our emotions are so intense that we might wonder whether our love can ever be returned in equal measure. We will endure the occasional hurt that is an inescapable component of any important relationship between lovers, parents and children, siblings, close friends. But that bit of pain within love does not diminish the value attached to following one's heart, for taking a chance to be more in life than just one person alone. Suffering one's love means allowing emotion with trust, despite the risk.

I was already praying for Frank every evening, and now it seemed that he need be gone only two or three days for me to begin worrying. He usually provided just a general description of where he would travel and was customarily vague about when he might return. Despite our conversation about Long An I did not know, had not the slightest idea of, what he did while away in other distant provinces. Once I asked him what his work was really all about and whether he was military or civilian. Was he trying to recreate a Long An experience in other provinces? He shrugged and replied that he only wanted to find answers to particular problems, and although he was not entirely military, many of his friends were.

He reminded me that his days and nights in Long An, more than anything else, made a convincing case for local forces operating from inside hamlets outward rather than the government working from outside to inward. That would be the best method, he thought, for competing with communists at the hamlet level. At the higher national level, South Viet Nam required a political program, a set of principles magnetically attractive to persuade people that the communist prescription was much less appealing by comparison. And the principles must be dynamically applied, not just printed on paper.

His answers were not entirely satisfactory for me because he was only one person and just an American. Who would be the Viet Nam leader who believed as he did? And even though he seemed guileless while speaking with me, I would realize a day or so later that I still knew little more about him than I had before we spoke.

I do remember that when there was a second military coup in late January, my Frank was in Lam Dong, an adjoining province, not in Dalat. He returned for only a day and then was away to Saigon again. We had only one night together, and I did not waste that time with speculation about which government general was on top of the new pile. There might be occasion for that when we would have more than a few hours together. But two days later, when Saigon radio broadcast an announcement of another new government and listed the names of sidelined generals who would be under house arrest in Dalat, I knew right away that I had a new personal problem.

The bantam boy general, Ton That Dinh—who once pursued me in Saigon—was one of those who would be shelved in my city; the lecherous General Tran Van Don who accosted me in the Bao Dai Palace several weeks earlier would be another! Although the sentences, announced with murky accusations by new military leader Nguyen Khanh, were for house arrest, I knew it would not be long before detention restrictions would be stretched to allow sorties to and around town. That meant that my harassers would eventually show up at my coffee shop and presume a warm welcome. I was glad my family no longer lived on the third floor.

Dalat was a strange sort of political game preserve because while Duong Van Minh remained in Saigon as nominal chief of state,[6] the other compromised generals were now a Dalat protected species, so long as they did not stray. The game warden was Colonel Dinh Van

---

[6] Duong Van Minh was the figurehead leader of the 1963 overthrow and murder of President Diem, pushed aside in 1964, but who in 1975 as head of a transitional administration surrendered Republic of Viet Nam armed forces to communist military representatives.

De, simultaneously province chief and mayor of our city. He was of the eclectic Cao Dai faith and may have been an uncontentious compromise alternative to appointing either a Buddhist or a Catholic. Colonel De was a smooth, apparently obsequious, multifaceted (I thought multifaced) administrator who bowed to Nguyen Khanh's moods and whims but who managed to express regard for the disgraced generals placed in his care. He probably could have just as easily acquiesced to a communist administration.

Thanks to having our own family villa, an address securable by a gate, and the probability that the sentence of "house arrest" would ensure that the exiles would not yet go anywhere in Dalat except for the market area, I was insulated from presumptuous generals. But I had not recalled that General Tran Van Don had a young son, Tran Van Thanh, who began to follow me like a puppy. That was manageable because he was just an awkward teenager, seven years younger than me. Fortunately, I was almost always in the company of the two friendly Dalat Academy instructors who kept a wary eye on each other and who acknowledged my special relationship, attachment really, with Frank.

And in spring 1964, Frank was mostly gone far away, usually in Quang Ngai and Binh Dinh Provinces, as he finally told me. That area was well known by all Vietnamese as a dangerous zone of intense communist activity in every district, and sometimes even within hamlets along coastal National Highway 1. Quang Ngai was the home province of Pham Van Dong, then prime minister of the communist government in the north. Frank was not so categorical, claiming instead that the two provinces had an interesting history and that there were good people in every part of Viet Nam.

When warned about the risk of road travel, Frank would always disagree, telling me and his friends that the roads he traveled were not as dangerous as people feared. I was not comforted, because he once returned to Dalat with a bullet hole in an upper corner of his jeep's windshield. On that occasion, he just shrugged off my suggestion that he underestimated the risks and soon found a garage on the edge of town that could install replacement glass. I loved him but knew he was a stubborn fool. I wondered whether he had been as evasive with his family and friends in America. Was he even now less than completely open with his supervisors? Whoever they were!

There were some comic episodes. Visitors occasionally arrived to speak with Frank, usually landing in small airplanes at the seldom used Cam Ly airstrip just outside of town. Once he needed to drive much further, to Lien Khuong Airport; because he was running late and hurrying, his office vehicle slid off the road and overturned. It was I who retrieved and brought him to his cottage where, to maid-cook Chi Bay's amusement, yours truly picked glass fragments from his tender rump before delivering my beloved to the "Soulier" Clinic.

Another time, his friend Talbot Huey, who worked further south in the Mekong area, visited from Saigon and later needed a ride to the Lien Khuong airfield. I volunteered to drive him in my car because Frank was committed elsewhere. My car got stuck in mud, it being the start of the rainy season, and Talbot, illogically for both of us, went to push from the rear to release us. Naturally a good part of the mud was sprayed on him by my spinning wheels!

Father, to my great dismay—because of the devastating effect on Mother—resumed his womanizing ways. He would stroll the streets uphill from our shop, walking around the market area, and befriend any lady, young or old, who might pay him attention in return for the implied gift of spending money. One day he announced the need to make a brief Saigon trip to check the condition of our old house. But I learned that he planned to meet a young Dalat waitress, with whom he had already made a liaison, expecting to have a good time in exchange for the promise of a few thousand piasters. Of course, those same thousands could only have been siphoned from our family business, but the theft did not anger me so much as his deceit and continuing disrespect of Mother.

Frank and me with Talbot Huey, who visited from Can Tho and later met us again in Saigon.

He took an Air Viet Nam flight. One day later I flew to Saigon and confronted them both. I bought off the poor girl, his prey, by conditionally providing her with more money than what my father had promised. The condition was her oath to keep away from my family and far from father in particular . . . forever. As for my father, would that I then had sufficient strength and ruthlessness to take a bamboo whip to him as he had to me when a little girl. But I cursed him in such a shame-inducing manner, so harshly, that we could barely be civil with each other for months afterward.

When next with Frank, I pestered him about wanting to see places that he was now more familiar with than I could be, even though this was my country, not his. I most wanted to travel north with him to the Central Viet Nam provinces. He would always, adamantly, insist that would not be possible because, first, the roads were now actually less safe than just a few months earlier, and second, he had to stay focused on the people, work, and teams for which he had responsibility. So, no compromise: I would not be allowed to share even just one long two- or three-day drive northward. Frustrated, I then insisted that at least out of consideration for our shared feelings he ought to tell me something more, something real, about what he was doing when gone for such long periods. His reply, that he was assisting friends to organize special units competing with communists in and around the Quang Ngai hamlets—similar to what he had done in Long An months before—was responsive but, as usual, still a touch too vague. However, that was all I could pry from him.

He did suggest, perhaps as a distraction, that I might like to accompany him to Saigon, and then to Vung Tau, where he would visit a special training camp. I was enthusiastic because my family (children and mother) would be able to make the trip. While it seemed to me that he was still being somewhat evasive, at least we would be together.

We drove to Saigon in a few hours, using our family Citroën rather than his jeep. The road from Dalat was still open, undisturbed by ambushes, and Frank even slept for an hour or so. When he woke, I asked what explanation should have been made if we had been stopped by unfriendly people. He suggested that I could insist to any obstructing party that he was my French husband.

"But your French is terrible!"

"Not a big problem," he said, "because I will just say that I come from a provincial place in Alsace where almost everyone speaks German."

"What if they question you in German?"

"Well," he smiled, "that would be a problem, but we're unlikely to encounter a German-speaking Vietnamese communist between Dalat and Saigon! And I know you would have thought of something!"

We were in Saigon only three or four days. A communist commando team somehow infiltrated the naval area along the river and placed charges at the waterline of a visiting American aircraft carrier. "That was a spectacular feat," we Vietnamese, even though anti-communist, thought among ourselves. When we met a few of his friends for dinner that evening, they were amused because the official American reaction per the press briefing was that, first, the ship was not actually an aircraft carrier: It was a former aircraft carrier, now used for transporting aircraft. Second, it had not been sunk because the keel merely submerged to rest on the river bottom; water never reached the flight deck. A Major Kelley, older than Frank but very familiar in his relationship, like an older brother or uncle, laughed and said that it was well for our side that the river was not deeper, or otherwise arguing "sunk or not sunk" would have been more absurd than it already was.[7]

The following day we were off to Vung Tau! The way to Vung Tau was toward Bien Hoa on the modern highway constructed with American economic assistance, and then a turn toward the coast. After passing Long Thanh, the road was generally through open terrain. To the right, but separated by intervening small farms and marshland, we were not far from the Saigon River. To the left were more small farms and then beyond, toward Xuan Loc, rubber plantations blending in the distance with some remaining forest cover. The road to Vung Tau was hardly ever—I am even tempted to say never—ambushed or otherwise interdicted by the communists. As with the route to Dalat, also frequently traveled by affluent Saigon residents and officials, it seemed that the communists wanted to avoid offending the very people they most scorned in propaganda.

Frank planned to spend most of a day at the training camp located not far from the highway and near the Vung Tau airfield. We would all be staying in a modest hotel for a couple of nights, with separate accommodations for mother, me, and my children, and another small room for Frank. We Vietnamese went to the market, fun for us, while someone came to take Frank away. I felt deprived of his company, but that proved fortuitous because the bumptious colonel of

---

[7] The former aircraft carrier-converted-to-aircraft-transport-ship was sunk to the point where the keel rested on the river bottom on May 2, 1964.

the Philippine embassy, habitué of reopened Saigon nightclubs and perennial pest, intercepted Mother and me at the market. He had learned from friends that I had just been in Saigon, and when he could not find me there, he guessed I might have come to Vung Tau.

He first almost desperately pleaded that he could not live without me. While Mother did not understand what he was getting at, my response was straight to the point. He would have to accept that he could never share life with me. I explained that men who fell in love with my voice when I sang were just falling in love with a dream imagined for themselves. And in that sense, they were really only in love with themselves, not me. To make myself perfectly clear, I loudly told him that if he continued to follow me or anyone in my family, if he were even within my sight, I would complain to the Vietnamese civil and military police headquarters in Saigon; then, diplomat or not, he would have difficulty with his own embassy. Although frustrated, even angry, he dared not risk his privileged position, shuffled off, and never bothered me again.

The next day, when we had a quiet moment on the beach, I told Frank about the unpleasant encounter, hoping he would not be jealous. He was not. Most solemnly, he explained, "We have something pretty good together; it feels true, just for ourselves. Nobody else counts. When we met in your coffee shop, I wasn't aware that you were a well-known singer and actress. But you are. So, people follow you, take photographs, speak with you. People in America who are celebrated in sports and entertainment have to manage those situations too. This has always—for a long time, anyway—been part of your public life, and it still is, especially with me usually far away. It could only be a problem for us if I did not believe you. A man who goes through life disbelieving the woman he cares for lacks self-confidence and trust in others. I am not that kind of person."

I was relieved to hear him speak of the unwelcome attention by other men as only a trifle, of no significance for us. Then, with concern for him and realizing that he had yet to mention anything about his meeting, I asked him whether our time in Vung Tau, aside from an hour or two on the beach with me, had been useful.

He replied that he had spent a few hours with two Vietnamese officers who ran the training camp. He was impressed with their character and commitment but also noticed that signs for different sections and camp areas were entirely in English. He thought it better to have all signs in Vietnamese and make Americans at the camp learn how to work within that language, rather than have Vietnamese in training take on the impression of foreigners controlling the center. Anyway, he went on, some of his friends who joined him in field training special units were now advocating, as he was practicing with them, a different approach: help organize local people, bring them straight into hamlets in their own districts for special instruction and training, practice working with people by day, and then defend the area and themselves at night.

That was just a little more than he had previously told me about what he and his friends were doing in Quang Ngai. Relieved, I supposed that he was perhaps not in as much danger as I sometimes feared, because he had just said that his work was about a different way of training. Foolish young woman that I was, I listened while he spoke but only heard—that is, believed—what I wanted, a very human trait.

Back in Dalat, after a day in Saigon transit, Frank was too soon gone northward again. Based on the fond illusion stemming from our talk in Vung Tau, I was not so worried as I would otherwise be had I known he was doing something more than training. I did not find out until after a few more months how mistaken I was. Just as well that my eyes were not fully open then. Because even when Frank was in Dalat for two or three days, my inescapable principal responsibility was still for my children. Of course, I wanted my mother and father in a balanced relationship, but I could not do that for them. I still believed the Dalat environment would be good for both parents, but my father was a long way from earning my

trust. Did I love him? Of course, I did; but after all that I had witnessed, above all my mother's frequent disappointment and hurt, I
was doubtful of his proclamations for personal reform. In addition
to worry about my parents, my three children were both a constant
joy and a constant concern, especially regarding their school performance and occasional mischief around the house.

A few weeks later, when Frank arrived "home" in Dalat, it seemed
to me that our previous travel by road to Saigon and Vung Tau had
been so effortless and absent of difficulty that I could once more
attempt to persuade him to bring me along when next driving north
to Binh Dinh, Quang Ngai, and even beyond to Hue. I was irritated
when he once more firmly refused. He was American and persisted
in driving roads that he said were not safe for me, a Vietnamese.
How much more arrogant could anyone be? And that is exactly how
I addressed him, accusing the man I loved of being a proud foreigner
who thought that he, from America, and in my country only two
years, already knew Viet Nam better than we Vietnamese. He was
discomfited, shifted his gaze almost boyishly, and explained that
not wanting to bring me north of Nha Trang was because he loved
me more each time we were together, and so would not risk my life
for anything. And, he continued, a risk it would surely be, no matter
what I might think or how long I could argue.

I reeled a bit at that confession—admission of love for me—but,
sharp-witted as always, I also plucked right from his own words a
possible compromise that would mean more time for us together,
and a new opportunity for learning about his work and the people
who were his distant vague partners. So, my immediate response
was to propose that we travel to Nha Trang but, as he had just said,
no further north. He hesitated but only briefly, a second or two, and
then responded that we could probably do Nha Trang and stay with
one of his friends who lived fairly close to the beach.

Before he could change his mind, I insisted that we set a date
for departure, because I would have to let my mother and Kim Chi

know the schedule. The sooner the better, I urged. Three days later we were on our way.

The road toward the coast was all twists and turns, and then from the Da Nhim dam to the Phan Rang forest an almost precipitous drop. We first turned north on Highway 1 and soon turned again onto the side road that runs to Cam Ranh Bay. There was a small café there at Ba Ngoi and we stopped for lunch. The scenery was beautiful and the countryside peaceful.

Arriving in Nha Trang, we drove along the beach avenue before turning by the Frigate restaurant and motel to arrive about a block further at our destination. Before leaving Dalat in his jeep that morning, Frank told me the friend hosting us was named Charley Fisher, and he was a civilian who repaired radio/telephone antenna equipment. I had no idea what that meant. But I was most surprised on arrival to find that Frank's friend was a Black American—or as we said in Vietnamese, *Nguoi My den*.

I had no feelings of racial prejudice; my surprise was due to assuming that, usually, "birds of a feather do really flock together." We Vietnamese usually cluster among ourselves, Cambodian Vietnamese would stick with their own, and mountain people stayed among their respective tribes with hardly any mixing. Frank and his friends were obviously very different.

Charley showed us to a bedroom that he explained was for guests and suggested we should all relax a bit in the living room before going for dinner later. But Frank and I decided to walk down to the beach instead, and we invited him to join us. There was a snack bar just across the beach road and right on the sand. We strolled over to relax with sugary lemonades. I was tired, more than expected, from bouncing along in the jeep for much of the day. So, it was soothing to finally be leaning back in a webbed chair, sipping lemon soda. I was content to let my thoughts drift while the two men spoke of the conditions for road travel, places where risks might be greater, and whether certain times of day at those points ought to be avoided. I may have napped as they talked; I do not remember.

The next morning when I woke—and for me that always means late in the morning—I looked out from the bedroom door; it was apparent Frank had already left. Charley was reading a book in the living room and, with a smile, said that Frank had told him I was a late riser. But he, Charley, would put together a plate of toast and a couple of eggs for me. After I quickly changed and freshened myself, a breakfast plate was waiting for me on the kitchen table, and Charley kept me company with what he said was only his third cup of coffee, so far.

I asked where Frank had gone. Charley said that when in Nha Trang, Frank would always visit people at the airfield, nothing unusual. Then he remarked that when arriving with Frank the previous day I had seemed surprised, and he wondered whether I was uncomfortable staying with someone like himself. This was the first time in my life that I was asked so directly about racial attitudes. I decided that the question, and Charley, deserved an equally direct and honest reply. So I told him, "Yes, I was surprised, but only because Frank could have told me so that I would have been prepared."

I have always remembered Charley responding that for as long as he had known Frank, he only paid attention to abilities, not appearance, because what a person can do is more important than what a person looks like. And, Charley continued, by not telling me anything before our arrival, Frank was assuming that I would not think any differently.

"That is so true," I told Charley. "But wouldn't some people feel uncomfortable with unfamiliar situations? Wouldn't most people feel surprised?"

"Yes," he replied. "Frank will definitely not hesitate to surprise people, and some might even be uncomfortable; but then, he doesn't care much about that."

Nha Trang beach, where I persuaded Frank to bring me by road north from Dalat.

So, during a late morning with eggs, toast, and coffee, I understood, from the perspective of his friend, something really important about Frank and me. We both viewed people as individuals, and we were both interested in what a person could do rather than with how they might be categorized by others. And I would think about this in a newly confirmed way.

In the afternoon, Frank and I walked down to the beach, swam, and played in the sand like children. When we took pictures with my camera, it seemed as though Frank could not be caught without a typical lens-shy frown; but I was smiling a lot.

The interlude in Nha Trang, once we returned to Dalat, seemed distressingly short. Barely two nights together in Charley's small cottage, a few hours on the beach, and then from Dalat, Frank was gone again. This time he was picked up by a small plane at the Cam Ly airfield and taken away to Pleiku for a regional meeting with the new American ambassador. I believe that was General Taylor.[8]

Meanwhile, I had to apply all my attention to a major conflict that flared between my father and my dear friend Kim Chi. My father always suspected, because Kim Chi was eyes and ears for me, that she was the person who had earlier revealed that he would slip away to Saigon for adventure with a compromised waitress. He had always wanted to be the general director for our coffee shop, but because I doubted his ability, knowing that his own Saigon enterprise had evaporated, I fended him off and away to a minor undefined vague role. But father was persistent, and insistent, that he be trusted with some management responsibility. Now he claimed that Kim Chi was not behaving correctly, that she allowed complimentary beverages much too often, and that she even took small amounts, beyond her salary, for herself.

Kim Chi was stricken by the unfair charges, and she was angry too. She told me that if did not feel as though she were trusted, she would leave for Nha Trang where friends had already invited her to sing in one of the military clubs. I was trapped by the conflict

---

[8] Ambassador Lodge, who signaled the green light to ambitious Vietnamese generals in August 1963, left Saigon in June 1964. He was replaced by General Maxwell Taylor, who obtained mixed results politically and presided over building a massive American military presence. When General Taylor left Viet Nam in July 1965, he was replaced by Henry Cabot Lodge! The second coming of Ambassador Lodge concluded in April 1967.

between them. I loved Kim Chi like a sister, but family is so paramount in Vietnamese culture that I could not cut off my father. So, he bullied his way, emotionally, toward driving a wedge between me and Kim Chi. My best friend was hurt, but she understood the impossibility of my favoring her over my disreputable father. Just as family consideration prevented President Diem from opposing his elder brother Archbishop Thuc and younger brothers Ngo Dinh Can and Ngo Dinh Nhu, less than one year after the Ngo family tragedy, I was likewise trapped within the web of family conformity as expected by Vietnamese culture. Kim Chi swore an oath with me that we would always be friends, and then she took the bus to Nha Trang. I suffered deeply for being separated from my young woman friend.

Father was triumphant, and I knew that from now on Mother and I would have to keep a close eye on expenditures and receipts. It was all too easy to read his glee and surmise his intent to pilfer monies to support an occasional escapade. Father was guileful, and between my distrust of him and my constant concern for my daughter Le Thu and the two boys, Bao and Khai, my own health was falling to pieces.

I was so weary that when Frank suggested we meet in Saigon while he attended some meetings, my first instinct was to stay in Dalat and keep an eye on my father and assure myself that our coffee shop would continue to be a successful enterprise. I knew that Frank would be driving to Saigon from one of the northward provinces, and because of the mid-1964 decline in highway security he was even less inclined to consider allowing me on the road with him. Most recently he had usually been accompanied by one of his local friends, a young Dalat-area tribesman named Toneh Ton, and so I was comforted by knowing that Frank would not be alone. Moreover, our traveling together, if he detoured to pick me up in Dalat, would at best place me in the back seat of the old, blue-painted jeep. Teeth-rattling and bone-warping discomfort would make me cranky: not good for a loving relationship. So, I flew to Saigon. I could usefully spend a few days there seeing some old friends who were suggesting that I return to Saigon and resume singing in the capital nightclubs.

Big surprise when we eventually met in Saigon! Frank was talking with one of the humanitarian assistance offices about selling the jeep. I had always thought the blue jeep was provided by the American government. He explained that he had brought his own jeep along when first coming to Viet Nam because he did not want the official issue of a vehicle used as a pretext to limit travel by road. But now he had concluded that travel in Central Viet Nam in mid-1964 was considerably more dangerous than it had been a year or two earlier.

He introduced me to a young Canadian doctor who had just accompanied him driving three days south from Quang Ngai. Frank left me with his friend after lunch, saying that he needed to go to the USIS downtown office to speak with his boss. Since I could not imagine anyone "bossing" him, I would have liked to go along to see that, but he only smiled and said, "Another time."

Frank's friend was Stan Frileck, a tall, handsome fellow who seemed to constantly smile and speak with animated eye-sparkling intensity. Stan told me that on the first day driving south, some shots were fired in the Duc Pho area where communist activity was frequent. Now they were planning to make a return trip in two or three days, right through the same location! Madness! Were all Frank's friends as crazy, as obstinate, as he? What about the sale of the jeep? Oh, Stan explained, his medical assistance organization would buy the jeep, and the paper transfer would be completed after yet one more return to Saigon by road!

It seemed to me that I always learned more about Frank from his friends than directly and openly from him. It was so frustrating for me because when we were face to face, whatever he planned to do would already have been determined before I would have an opportunity to express an opinion. So now, only from Stanley Frileck did I learn that he planned to sell the jeep because road travel was much more risky north of Nha Trang than previously. Okay! But before actually turning the jeep over to a new owner, he would make one more drive, with his equally crazy friend, back through the same area where they had just escaped an ambush. Then, some days later, he would run the gauntlet once more on a final drive back to Saigon, after having acknowledged how dangerous the road was!

Two days later, the men were jeep-mounted and northward bound. I flew back to Dalat, trying to console myself by thinking the two friends were perhaps more careful than I had dared believe. There might even be some small chance they actually knew what they were doing. Anyway, while my opinion might have carried some weight if strongly expressed, in the end Frank and his friend would probably still go their own way, and always by road!

CHAPTER 7

Love Strained

O ur family finances, I found on my return to Dalat, were a sticky
tangle of unresolved debt, unorganized receipts for the coffee
shop income, and a stack of overdue bills perpetually set aside
by my father rather than paid. How deeply I regretted his having
chased my friend Kim Chi far away to Nha Trang, unjustifiably
accusing her of what he was most probably guilty of himself. Mother
and Father were constantly either arguing about his resumption of
seeking out other women and providing them with gifts purchased
from our family resources or staring each other down in sullen
silence. I knew then that, having yielded to Father's pressure because
of family loyalty, I had undermined my own greater family interests
by sending away my best friend.

I felt then, in September 1964, that too many people were
financially dependent on me. Father was sending small amounts of
money every month to his relatives in Saigon, as evidence of his own
supposed business success in Dalat. We had to pay not only the staff
in the coffee shop but also a family driver and gardener at our small
villa. And, of course, there was always school tuition due for Le Thu,
Bao, and Khai. The bills never stopped, and they even seemed to
increase from month to month. I knew that Kim Chi would not be

willing to return to Dalat, but thinking that she might have suggestions, I sent a note to her by Frank, hand delivered, when he transited Nha Trang on his way to who knew where. She quickly replied by letter that although my parents were now totally dependent on me, my father would always be manipulative, to the point that his emotional trickery could prevail even over the welfare of my children. She suggested the only solution would be to break away from my father; but she understood how difficult, probably impossible, that would be, because Mother would always side with Father, no matter how despicable his transgressions against her.

Tortuously chewing on the problem for several days, I concluded that since the ownership of our coffee shop did not provide the mooring point for family stability that I had hoped, perhaps the best option would be to sell the shop, retain the villa and keep the children in Dalat schools under my parents' care, and return to Saigon and resume my singing career for a consistent income. During recent travel to Saigon with Frank, old friends and club owners had urged me to do exactly that, and they insisted that my coming back to sing would provide even more money than previously. But Dalat, in my heart, would always be the mountain home where I first connected with Frank. It seemed essential to stay in the one place where we could occasionally share time without distraction. Impossible, I thought, to find a solution balancing the family's financial needs with my heartfelt desire to frequently, or at least once every few weeks, see Frank.

I needn't have had to vacillate. When Frank was next in Dalat for a few days, he told me that he would soon transfer southward from Central Viet Nam to work in districts close to Saigon. So, he would vacate the small Dalat cottage where we had shared precious moments. Although he thought some sort of temporary housing would be arranged in the Saigon area, there was no commitment from the embassy. Just as soon as he shared that news, and it did seem to happen quickly, Frank left again on his way northward to bid farewell to those with whom he had worked for most of the last two years. And so, I scrambled to make sense, at least organization-ally, of my own move to Saigon. I still planned, most definitely, after selling the coffee shop, to keep my small house in Dalat. Mother and Father could maintain the property and care for my children while the latter continued school. I thought I could persuade Kim Chi—eventually if not right away—to leave Nha Trang and join me in Saigon to be a companion and manager of finances. She and my father would be well separated, having no reason to meet, and I really needed a smart, trustworthy friend in the Saigon environment.

We found a buyer for the coffee shop. Because we had a steady clientele and a good local reputation, we did not lose money. In fact, the alacrity with which the sale was closed seemed to confirm that the recent financial difficulty was due to my father's income diver-sion. The transaction provided what I thought might be sufficient money to contract for a small house in Saigon. We did not have enough to buy into that inflating real estate market, but I hoped a secure long-term lease would be possible.

I had many old friends in Saigon. One introduced me to Nguyen Thi Hai, an attractive and obviously quick-witted woman who worked in the police advisory office of the US Agency for International Development (USAID). Mrs. Hai was a multitalented dabbler in real estate who knew my name as a popular singer and occasional actress. She seemed fascinated by the prospect of our being friends. Mrs. Hai showed me different housing possibilities, and I wasted no time in selecting a small two-story dwelling that, in fact, she owned. 185 Truong Minh Giang Street was down a narrow dirt drive, paralleling a small stream that was one of many polluted urban tributaries eventually joining the Saigon River.

At first, I sang for the Hotel Majestic nightclub on the top floor, then Maxim's and Ma Ca Ban. I traveled from venue to venue in small, blue-and-cream-colored Saigon taxis. Soon the Rex rooftop restaurant was added to my schedule. I understood that the Rex was now an American officers' club but was surprised to see that Americans, everywhere, comprised the primary audience and customer base throughout Saigon in restaurants and on all the small shop streets like Nguyen Hue, Hai Ba Trung, and Tu Do. It was not as though Vietnamese had completely disappeared, but we were actually displaced, to an observable extent, by Americans with a greater amount of money. There had always been a black market in currency exchange, dating to the French colonial period, and now the American dollar was so much in demand that the official exchange rate was generally ignored by both nationalities. Americans and their friends had the dollars and benefited accordingly.

Audiences warmly received my return, were even enthusiastic, especially American soldiers far from home responding to familiar nostalgic songs: "I Left My Heart in San Francisco," "Love is a Many-Splendored Thing," "I Can't Stop Loving You," and other titles that stirred memories. Occasionally men would proffer flowers and gifts, sometimes following my taxi from one club to the next. Soon I found it best to enlist two Vietnamese girlfriends to accompany me and so buffer my escape from one location onward to the next. I maintained a gracious smile for all, even while my heart yearned for the days that the man I loved would, too seldom, appear in Saigon.

Finally, the American embassy provided Frank a small three-room townhouse in the Tan Binh District, an urbanized area between Saigon proper and Tan Son Nhut Airport. Surprisingly, but happily, the adjoining home was occupied by Douglas Ramsey, he who had introduced us more than a year earlier. Knowing Frank was housed side by side with a mutual friend comforted me, even though I still did not understand what they were doing, separately, together, or with others. I cared only that I personally benefitted from Frank and his friends working in the Gia Dinh districts adjacent to the city. We could see each other more frequently than when he had been hundreds of kilometers away in the central provinces.

And who were those friends of his? I remember one in particular, Do Minh Nhat, northern Vietnamese by accent. Once while I was waiting for Frank at his newly assigned house, Nhat told me that many years earlier some Americans provided him special training (on an island far away, he said), then he worked for a university research team and later, after joining the American information service, worked with Frank in some Long An Province hamlets. Ah, the mystery of those hamlets in Long An! I asked Nhat what he and Frank had really done the previous year in Long An. He replied that it was all about visiting every family in a hamlet, being friendly, asking people how they lived and how they survived amidst a contest between the government and communists. Of course, he continued, sometimes they encountered small communist teams trying to embed themselves into that same area. Now, Nhat explained, he and a few others were working with American friends to help people in the hamlets west of the airport to organize a local defense force special unit. I suggested that, so close to Saigon, the area must already be fairly safe. Nhat laughed and replied that in recent months one need not go far from the city to bump heads with communists.

And how about Frank's American friends? Eventually I met most of them. The names were, for this child of Viet Nam, not easy to fix in the mind. I created simple nicknames because too many new faces meant that complete names, given and family, were impossible for me to recollect. Frank's boss, although their relationship seemed more like that of uncle and nephew, was called Ev. There was another sort of uncle named Vann (at first, I thought his name was our common "Van" spelled with one "n"), a third uncle figure I remembered from before as "Kelly from Quang Ngai." There were two special forces captains named Werbiski and Drinkwater (who for memory aid I thought of as "whiskey" and "*uong nuoc*"—the latter of which was simply a literal translation to Vietnamese). Two other captains I recall as Mad and Mac.

I wish that I could give you every name, because when I close my eyes, I can bring them all, at least their images, to mind, even after more than fifty years. Others included Luong from somewhere near Hue who had been Viet Minh, Tri from the far south, and an American walking with a limp, but always smiling, "Joe" or "Joey V." There were sergeants, one named Lonnie. How could I distinguish a sergeant? Well, they would occasionally, but not always, casually salute. There was nothing servile about relations within their circle. Saluting was something like an informal acknowledgment: "I heard you, and I'm taking care of that."

Another older American would occasionally meet with them. That was Ralf Jonson from the CIA. And how did I know that? Because, dear readers, he told me. And I did not even know what those letters meant, except that Ralf seemed to think them important, because when he pronounced them, he lowered his voice as if sharing something secret. Readers will think me naive, and truly I was.[9]

Frank was also meeting some of my friends, because when he was able to come to Saigon, initially about once a week or so and later more infrequently, we could attend a Vietnamese *cai luong* (renovated theater) performances or art exhibitions. Kim Chi left

[9] Almost sixty years have passed. Most of these men are gone now. Everett Bumgardner, spark plug and one-time executive assistant to William Colby, died in 2005 in Virginia. When Frank walked away from me in 1966, Everett sympathetically advised me to just let him go until the war was over. John Paul Vann and Frank were entwined one way or another until John Vann was killed in a helicopter crash near Kontum in 1972. He is the subject of a biographical study by Neil Sheehan. John had married the daughter of my next-door neighbor in Dalat, and they had a child of their own. Phil Werbiski, one of Frank's closest friends, was killed in Laos in 1969. He is buried in Illinois, and someday we will visit that cemetery. Jim Drinkwater, Joe Vaccaro, Lonnie Johnson, Ralf Jonson, and Gordon Huddleston have all moved far beyond our limited horizon. Phan Manh Luong, once Viet Minh, died in a California Buddhist monastery. Do Minh Nhat passed on in Virginia. Only one of that band, Tran Huu Tri of the Republic Army 43rd Rgt. and subsequently with Frank and friends, lives still in Georgia. Charley Fisher is last known to have taken a medical aide assignment in Beirut. No one has seen him recently. He may yet be simply far away, laughing at the follies of men and women.

Nha Trang and returned to Saigon as my most constant dependable friend. I never knew when Frank might arrive at my door. When he did, my heart would soar, but my personal pride when in the presence of Vietnamese guests would always constrict my demonstrative glee; so, I would introduce him to others only as an American friend whom I had met in Dalat. Perceptive writers, especially those tuned in to the world of film and nightclubs, like Trong Minh, might have privately concluded otherwise. But all those who guessed my true sentiments were discreet, and no one belittled me for loving an American. When he was in Saigon for a day or two, I would go to his small house in Tan Binh and stay the night with unrestrained love.

My new contract agreements for nightly singing engagements were with venues whose owners remembered my singing two years previously. Needing income to continue supporting my parents and children in Dalat and to cover Saigon expenses, I soon added the Kon Tiki nightclub, located in the Da Kao area, close by the point of entry for the Bien Hoa Highway. One customer, Ngo Viet Thu, a well-known Saigon urban planner, would always request my version of "The Blue Danube" (Dong Song Xanh); although the performance was exhausting for me, patrons had to be accommodated.

It seemed to everyone that my time away in Dalat had somehow strengthened and sweetened my voice. Word spread even more rapidly than I would have thought possible. I was besieged by other club and restaurant owners who offered large sums of piasters for each nightly set of three or four songs. My ability to sing a few American songs spurred popularity, but in every appearance, I also included nostalgic Vietnamese songs like "Noi Long" and "Dem Dong."

Every morning I would practice for about one hour, then after eating fresh fruit brought from the market by Kim Chi, I would rest in the afternoon before preparing to sing again. Despite the resulting fatigue, I needed consistent income because, per a revised agreement with Nguyen Thi Hai, I purchased the house that she originally provided on lease. I was even able to buy a secondhand automobile and pay a driver to deliver me from venue to venue and finally home. It was an expense, true, but safer to have my own transportation for evading admirers who might attempt to suborn taxi drivers and so easily follow me from club to club, and maybe even to my home.

On those few precious evenings, far too few for me, when Frank was in Saigon, he would come to hear me sing, usually at the Majestic or Ma Ca'Ban. As soon as I would see him, my next song, no matter what had been fixed with the band, would be "Noi Long" (*yeu ai, yeu ca mot doi*); he knew that the meaning (who do I love, the one that I love my whole life) was especially for him. Frank would almost always be with two or three of his (what some might have thought rough-looking) Vietnamese and American friends. But they looked fine to me, and I understood them to be like brothers. They were polite, unexpectedly quiet compared to other nightclubbing patrons, and always seemed uncomfortable in the Saigon milieu, as if they ached to return to the hamlets, rice paddies, and trails in the woods.

Among themselves, while I might sit with Frank, they would murmur of Rung Sat, Cho Dem, Nhi Binh, a few places not far from Saigon that I recalled from when I worked with civic action— but names of places that I was sure no well-dressed Saigon American, and even few Vietnamese, could recognize, much less have visited. Frank and I were closer geographically than we had been in previous months when he was somewhere far north of Nha Trang and I was business- and family-bound in Dalat. Yet, even then I knew—that is, truly understood—nothing more than what he and his friends told me, and their descriptions were, no doubt deliberately, vague.

Until spring 1965, the American military presence had been either advisory or specialized. I even thought of Frank and his friends as advisors, maybe leading on occasion, but fundamentally looking for the right people, and always supporting, maybe even stimulating, local initiatives. Some obvious American specialization was in aviation. I knew the helicopters were primarily American but also learned that a few Americans were flying missions, not just advising the Republic of Viet Nam Air Force.

An enormous change in the war, amounting to a gravitational shift, took place that spring when regular—not advisory, not specialized, but in fact big American military formations, divisions, and regiments—were placed in Viet Nam. Even in Saigon, insulated from countryside conflict, this was understood to be necessary for staving off increasingly assertive communists who, as evidenced by their own battalions and newly organized regiments, were threatening to knock over successive self-cannibalizing South Viet Nam administrations. The increasingly more aggressive self-named South Viet Nam Liberation Front, organized in greater numbers than before, and at least as well armed as government soldiers, was ascendant not only in a few distant provinces but, more alarmingly, in districts not far from the capital.

In cafés and coffee shop venues like Brodard and Givral, and in all their competitor shops along broad avenues and down alleyways, everyone was talking about the change. Even those who previously rued an increasing foreign presence—the American swagger on Saigon streets—now counted on them, despite increased traffic sometimes including truck convoys through the heart of our capital and rising prices for rents and commodities, to act as a *deus ex machina* in the saving of our country!

I felt apprehensive. My country, my people, all of them—including Cambodians and members of the hill tribes, as well as Vietnamese of the three regions—I knew from personal experience did not fit easily together. One common trait among most of us, though, was a contempt for the colonial French; now another foreign power, well-intentioned but still foreign, would be killing some of us. With what purpose? What goal? And to fulfill whose dream?

More than anything, I wanted to talk with Frank, because his awareness of the problem was deeper than that of anyone else with whom I might share private thoughts. But Frank and his friends were far away, at first in Long An and then even further to Sa Dec and Vinh Long. I knew from one of them, transiting Saigon, that their numbers were increasing, not only by adding a few Americans but also because they sometimes enlisted a talented combatant identified during training. They allowed a few *chieu hoi* (former communist adherents) to join, and even induced three of the captured enemy to work with them in supporting local forces opposing the communist party.

At last, Frank returned to Saigon. On the first day we had lunch and a long sensual afternoon. I anticipated a few days' reunion and prayed for more than that. On the second day, then, I was shocked when he returned from a meeting and told me that he was now required, in a few days, to take leave back to America. "Home leave" might seem advisable, perhaps especially in his own instance, because years passed in another country, especially one at war, may alter a young man's sense of belonging. But if home is really "where the heart is," then Viet Nam was in fact his real home. However, nothing else would do but yield to accepted practice. And there was, I thought, an exciting possibility for travel together that could provide me the opportunity to meet his family. I took Frank to a well-known tailor shop downtown to supervise measurements and the selection of fabric for a complete suit. When he greeted his mother, a new gentlemanly appearance would demonstrate that I not only loved her son but would care for him.

Such an optimistic perspective, my dream, was dashed when my application for a passport was denied. The intricacies of Tran Le Xuan family law, enacted a few years previously during the Ngo family administration, had not yet been modified. So, although I was legally separated and independent, until officially divorced I could not receive my own passport. Rather than be curdled sour, I decided that after Frank left for his solo travel to America—and had returned—I would contract legal assistance to do whatever was necessary to finally obtain an unlimited complete divorce. Months later, on October 16, 1965, I did receive that certificate of freedom and independence.

A handful of days flew by, and then Frank was gone. I could not bid him farewell at Tan Son Nhut Airport; a public parting would be observable trauma. One of his friends took him by jeep, and as they drove away, I realized that he always seemed to be drawing away from me.

So now he was, hour by hour, further and further from Viet Nam, on wings to his own country. I knew, just absolutely knew, that had we been able to travel together I would have not only symbolically but also indivisibly joined his family, and those few days would have bound us forever. Our circle would be complete, with no possible disconnect. Of course, I understood that Frank would surely return, and not just for me but for the war as well—that complicated, multidimensional, kaleidoscopically shimmering, fearsome magnet that drew him and his friends, absorbing them, into hamlets and woods, searching for a winning formula.

Yes, I realized, even then, that the complexity of war was slowly but surely enveloping him, but this war was in my country. Just as he could not withdraw permanently from Viet Nam, so too he would forever be connected to me. I knew, with complete certainty, that he would always return. I was inseparably part of the life that mattered most to him. And, just as surely as I was part of his Viet Nam world, in the same way he was part of mine.

CHAPTER 8

Love Eclipsed

I was in stasis—a sort of deep sleepwalking, as though in a semi-conscious state—for those three or four weeks while Frank was with family and friends in America. But my own Viet Nam was increasingly restless. Every province was racked by communist agitation and much more frequent guerrilla attacks. Northeast of Saigon, and farther north in Central Viet Nam, major communist military attacks, combined with inadequate response, caused the retraction of a government presence to district towns and province capitals. The wobbly administration presided over by the new prime minister, air force pilot and general officer Nguyen Cao Ky, could not cope on its own.[10] There was no alternative but to accept an increase in the number of American military formations, advisors, and logistics specialists as the only feasible way to offset the impact of expanded communist operations now reinforced, like steel rods, by new regular army units sent south by the Hanoi government.

Saigon was no longer immune to developments. In March, while Frank had been somewhere south of the Mekong, the American

---

[10] Nguyen Cao Ky, Viet Nam Air Force officer whose northern Viet Nam origin limited his ability to develop bonds of loyalty. Despite that handicap, he succeeded in becoming prime minister during the 1964–1966 period of nonconstitutional government.

embassy in downtown Saigon was shattered by a car bomb deto-
nated on the adjacent street. There were injuries and losses of life
(Americans and Vietnamese); afterward, everyone understood that
a new feature of conflict would be extending the war into central
Saigon. Late June, just before Frank returned, the My Canh floating
restaurant, in the line of sight of and not many steps from the Hotel
Majestic, was bombed. We all knew it was targeted because of being
a favorite of Americans and their Vietnamese friends.

A nervous reaction was immediately observable. The venues
where I sang each evening now hired security guards to serve as a
minimal preventive measure, even if only by being obvious at entry-
ways. It was never clear, and fortunately not tested, as to whether
armed doormen made a prophylactic difference or not. Likewise,
draping wire screening over plate-glass windows and open-air
seating areas may have deterred grenade throwers, or simply adver-
tised an ongoing vulnerability. In either case, no one chose, or was
ordered, to throw explosive devices for quite some time.

Frank returned in late July. At just about the same time, in a
revealing incident demonstrating that Americans might be almost as
inflammatory as the French, Nguyen Thi Hai, from whom I bought
our Saigon house, was killed by a jealous American boyfriend. She
was working in the Public Safety Division within USAID, the office
responsible for Americans advising and supporting Vietnamese
police. Saigon newspapers swarmed this story, reporting that an
enamored American advisor killed another American who was
head of the public safety advisory office. The shooter then immediately killed Mrs. Hai. Whether the second murder was from prox-
imate rage or an insane reaction to betrayal could not be known.
She had not been my close friend, but it was impossible to refrain
from feeling sympathetic grief for her fate and the consequences for
her children. Many times during the next few years I thought of
the Nguyen Thi Hai murder as a metaphor for the worst behavior
of both nationalities. Some Vietnamese were tempted to set moral

behavior aside to obtain access to American largesse, while some Americans enjoyed pursuing women and playing games for personal benefit within semi-imperial circumstances.

But Frank had finally returned. I was, admittedly, deliriously happy for the few days and nights that he was in Saigon. Some of his friends joined us in restaurants, and a few accompanied him to hear me sing. By day, while I rested, he was making a circuit of the offices that seemed to influence, if not absolutely determine, his assignments in Viet Nam. Too soon, a decision came down in some mystifying manner that he ought to be off to Chau Doc Province. I knew, of course, that meant he would be not far from the Cambodian border, but the area was predominantly Hoa Hao by religious persuasion, and the Hoa Hao were probably the most anti-communist group in Viet Nam. I was relieved, until I learned from one of his friends that they would be working outward from a special forces camp in the An Phu District. I knew from my civic action experience in years past that An Phu was its own singularity by, cartographically speaking, poking like a finger into Cambodia.

So, now that I was better informed, my sense of relief evaporated as Frank went off to the far south with special forces friends, those Americans and several Vietnamese connected to them during the past two years. There was nothing I could do but let him know that I would always be waiting, and then each night . . . pray. I was totally unsuspecting of the slightest possibility or even appearance of his straying from our shared bond of love, loyalty, and concern for each other. The strangest part of his bringing another woman to his Saigon house in the late summer, then, is that he actually told me he would do so!

When he first returned from Chau Doc, and after having described with some enthusiasm the hamlets and people of the border area, Frank told me that on his next return to Saigon there would be a young lady with him. She was, he explained, the niece of an important province official and would be applying for a job in Saigon. He had been asked to assure her safety while in the city. Once she left to return to her family in Chau Doc, he would reconnect with me. On the surface this seemed plausible to me, in the context of everything transpiring in my country. But as always in Viet Nam, and especially within every personal relationship, beware of what might be percolating underneath! What is being filtered and to whose advantage?

I only knew precisely which day he returned about two weeks later, with the young lady, because the sometimes housemaid and cook I had met previously in Dalat, Chi Bay, sent a message to me. She rather vehemently urged me to come to Frank's house and call out for her at the rear kitchen entrance. Ah, Frank, my love, so competent in hamlets, forest, and along trails, but so foolish to assume that Chi Bay's loyalty to him would be primary, when in fact her bond with me as a Vietnamese woman would always be stronger. So, after I drove to that small house that I knew so well, and sitting in the kitchen with Chi Bay, we both heard Frank speaking politely and almost as warmly as he most often did with me, but now with a Chau Doc girl. Chi Bay, frowning and with gritted teeth, went back and forth to bring dishes from the kitchen and later clear the table. I could hear host and guest speaking but did not understand exactly what was said. Soon Frank escorted the visiting woman upstairs.

I knew, intimately, that there were two bedrooms above: the one that we sometimes shared, and another for guests. Chi Bay, eyes flaring, insisted that I climb the stairs and confront the two who had just shared a meal and now might be sharing something else. We two friends exchanged pushes and shoves, as I refused to do that. I would not be the actress in a real-life tragedy or comic farce.

Eventually, we were at a stalemate. I walked outside to my car, determined to drive back to my own house. Just before unlocking the car door, in a sudden-onset reaction from having resolutely sat to eavesdrop with Chi Bay, I began to softly sob. Feeling weak from the neck downward entirely through the length of my spine, I almost collapsed. I could barely turn the key, start the ignition, release the parking brake, and, with heart aching, make my way home.

Frank had strayed to some degree—crossed a fence, as he might have put it—even if only on the face of it; but to what extent? I was personally hurt and felt cut to the heart; perhaps not betrayed, but sort of trampled upon. However, not having witnessed what had followed the dinner and therefore unable to be sure of whether there had been physical intimacy, I decided not to speculate about what might have, but should not have, been done. But although aching, and angry too, I would not discard my connection to the man I loved with an intensity and commitment impossible with any other. But now wounded, my trust was diminished.

In this respect, looking back too many years, it seems I could have been replicating the behavior of my mother, repeating a family pattern that sacrificed personal honor for stability in a relationship. In fact, this seems to be a too frequent and painful response for many of us. We tolerate pain, personal slight, disparagement, an emotional stab to the heart, then rationalize the entire situation while disregarding the indignity. All in an attempt to hold on to a relationship that may be failing, but the failure of which would be even more destructive to our sense of self.

The next day Frank appeared at my house, telling me that the young woman visitor had stayed only one night and had already departed for Chau Doc. He seemed blithely unaffected by what may have been a questionable interaction between them; and I, although not yet acclaimed as the best Viet Nam actress, instinctively played my own smiling but cool part in what may have been a deceptive exchange for both of us. I wondered, even as he with apparent innocence spoke, whether an ability for subterfuge and deceit was inherent to all men. Or, had Frank been so trained by his mentors, in preparation for missions abroad, to skillfully apply the dark arts of deception and misdirection, that now they were second nature?

There are so many dissimilarities between men and women that enumerating them requires volumes, hours of discussion within each relationship, and a mutual sense of humor. One of those differences, experienced by all of us, has to do with shopping. The very word implies, for women, browsing, leisurely examining things (often with no firm commitment to purchase), looking around, a willingness to be distracted by any item just noticed. For us women, shopping is an experiential venture with the associative health benefit of slow walking. Men do not "go shopping." Men go somewhere to buy, with focus (or one could say with narrow-mindedness), one or two things. If more than one or two things are needed, they will make a list—not so much to avoid forgetting the important but rather to refrain from any time-consuming distraction that we women might find interesting.

More relevant to my situation with respect to Frank, and to be borne in mind by all women, is that we want to be loved whereas men generally want to love. We want to be understood, appreciated. Men want to appreciate, to pursue. Women are prepared for a family focus—not that a career beyond family is impossible, but for most women at some point in our lives, family will be prime. Men are more easily tempted to look beyond family. I remember Frank having told me that his own father, over the age for military draft service in World War II, did not want to be considered lacking in patriotism, so he insisted on volunteering for the Army, thereby abandoning his wife and two young sons. He followed his country's flag and his own conscience, never to return, killed on a European battlefield. Frank felt his father's act a noble one. I thought his mother would not have shared that sentiment.

I do understand there is a real difference between men looking, with curiosity, at women, distinct from gazing upon a woman with lustful intent, ready to make a physical connection if there seems the slightest possibility. I am also aware of the case sometimes made for evolutionary imperative: that because our ancestors comprised a few lonely clans moving outward from Africa around seventy thousand years ago, and because they were seen as prey by sharp-toothed and sharp-clawed mammals, the survival of our species would be enhanced by mating as frequently as possible. I do not know how scientific, or generally accepted, that theory, but it is sometimes proffered as a rationalization for contemporary male misbehavior. Even if that evolutionary purpose, the survival of species, was the factor that energized promiscuous male behavior, can we not evolve to a new model, one of mutual respect within a family-nurturing relationship? Can we temper the primeval instinct? Can we achieve moral metamorphosis?

I have thought a great deal about this issue. But at that point of my hurt in late summer 1965, I was still sure in my heart that Frank had only unwittingly strayed by appearance, not in actuality. I knew, very deeply in my soul, that he would never betray me. Our relationship was so special that he could never find an equivalent; no other woman, for him, could match me. So thinking, I submerged myself in what can be described as a tendency of women in love to rationalize, to a greater extent than you would expect, a loved one's thoughtless, careless behavior.

I never told him what was observed, surmised, suspected. Whenever I thought of that evening, an uncomfortable intent to separate from him crept within my heart. I did not tell anyone, not even Kim Chi. The hurt was mine. The problem was mine.

Two days passed, a time for me to practice self-control and for him to run around Saigon to meetings—to what purpose, I never asked. Too soon for me, for my emotional equilibrium, he was on his way by road back to Chau Doc. I was only comforted, even amid my usual concern for his safety, by knowing Frank was still south of the Mekong. I am a southern woman, by accent and social identity. We southerners—a mix of Vietnamese, Cambodians, relaxed southern Buddhists, southern Catholics, Hoa Hao, Cao Dai—are generally more practiced in accommodation than citizens of the central and northern provinces. Moreover, if necessary, so long as he was somewhere in my home region, I would know how to find him. Even the major roads south of Saigon were usually safe, at least by day. The sharper, more deadly, engagements were all to the north of Saigon.

So, of course, by some ironic twist of fate, several days later Frank returned and, after meeting with whoever controlled his assignments, shared some startling news with me. He would stay connected with American special forces and bring some Vietnamese cadre back north to Binh Dinh and Quang Ngai. He thought it adequate clarification to tell me that he was still only on loan with special forces. On loan? What did that mean? My being startled proves that even after two years, despite having heard descriptions of what had been organized west of Saigon several months earlier, I truly understood little of what he was doing. What organization, what office, really sponsored him? When we met in Dalat, he had told me that he was a civilian and a foreign service officer. But if he were truly civilian, why was he unlike others? How was it that a combination of different offices would send him and his friends—with most of those friends being military, not civilian—here and there? And if he and the others were actually military in civilian disguise, how could they speak and act so independently?

I knew the Central Viet Nam provinces were more dangerous than those of the south, and they were also beyond my reach. Road travel beyond Dalat and Nha Trang was now at extreme risk. The southern population was conglomerate and relatively inclined to accommodate. The central population was fractious and did not shirk confrontation. The accent of their speech was stronger than my own southern voice. They were sometimes as antagonistic to us of the south as they were to people of the north. The Buddhists of Hue and Danang, it seemed to us in Saigon, were militant and intolerant relative to those of the south. After just a couple of months in Chau Doc, my Frank had affiliated with Hoa Hao Buddhists. He explained to me that he appreciated the emphasis placed on an individual commitment to principles of ethical behavior, meditation, and an absence of priestly hierarchy. That was all fine with me: better to have an attachment to some spiritual values than none at all. But how would those Buddhists of Qui Nhon, who knew him two years earlier, now feel about the young American Hoa Hao convert?

I was sure Frank understood more about Viet Nam than any other foreigner, but a 60 percent comprehension was nothing like the 90 percent or more that he presumed to possess. A year earlier Frank had traveled to, and had even done some organizing and training in, those provinces very distant from Saigon, and so I acknowledge that he knew more of all the land beyond Nha Trang than I did. But the situation now, in late 1965, was very different from that which had existed only twelve months earlier.

The communist party introduced regular army units from North Viet Nam into border regions of Central Viet Nam. Those were just the first of what would eventually be many. In Saigon, although comparatively insulated from the developing new reality, we understood that the situation in Central Viet Nam was worse than ever before. How could we Saigon citizens be so aware of the recent, but distant, frightening circumstances? First, we had a healthy skepticism of the official reports provided for radio broadcast and publication in newspapers; and second, there were always soldiers on leave or wounded in hospitals who shared the bitter truth with family members.

Our country was especially vulnerable just then because of the political drift from 1964 through 1965. The scoundrels who betrayed Ngo Dinh Diem in November 1963, murdering the very president who had placed stars on their collars, had been shuttled off to Dalat in early 1964 by newly ascendant, perpetually scheming, General Nguyen Khanh. Now little more than a year later Nguyen Khanh, inept manipulator, was pushed from center stage and replaced by General Nguyen Cao Ky, with General Nguyen

Van Thieu in waiting,[11] and General Nguyen Chanh Thi observant from far-off Danang and Hue. What a spiderweb of intrigue! We in the Republic of Viet Nam must have appeared to be building a house of straw. And, as in a certain nursery rhyme, the big bad Hanoi wolf planned to blow our house down.

The man I loved, so deeply that he was forgiven for his inattention, was now where the expanding war was more intense than in any other part of my country. Most of his friends, both American and Vietnamese, were gone with him. No longer did I see the familiar faces of those in his circle in the nightclubs where I sang. No news, I argued within myself, was at least not bad news. Then after several weeks he was back for three days. The small Tan Binh house previously provided for his use had been reassigned when Frank was sent north. Now while in Saigon he had a small bedroom reserved for his use in an embassy residence. I didn't care where we ended up; it was just good to lie close beside him again.

But that November 1965, Frank was uncharacteristically grim, had lost much weight, and seldom smiled. More accurately, I do not recall him smiling at all. He only seemed to relax when I asked him about the friends who followed him, Vietnamese and Americans. Some were familiar to me, others were new. Too soon—it felt like a matter of hours—he was gone off and away again. There had not been any opportunity to let him know that the previous month I finally obtained a divorce and was now free for marriage with him. I did not want to appear as though forcing a commitment, and I also sensed that Frank might be drifting, drifting away from me, lost in some fog of miserable conflict. I could be his anchor if he would let me. I knew that no other woman could measure against me, but I had not foreseen that most dangerous of bewitching sirens: an

[11] Nguyen Van Thieu, born in Phan Rang of the central region, eventually outmaneuvered Nguyen Cao Ky to become president of the Second Republic of Viet Nam in 1967 and achieved reelection in 1971. He departed Saigon for England in 1975 and later relocated to the Boston area in America, where he died in 2001.

insistent whispering of brotherhood in war, a collective risk and sacrifice for a noble cause.

We did not meet, and could not share love, during Christmas and New Year of 1966. I received no message and had no idea where Frank might be. One day I encountered a Vietnamese army officer in Cho Ben Thanh, the central Saigon market, and he told me that Frank had brought two wounded soldiers to the clinic where his sister worked somewhere in Binh Dinh Province. I could not control my tears. We used to say that our country was like a village wherein sooner or later you would meet someone who knew your family. But secondhand reports of a loved one in probable danger could not be anything but painful.

Later in January my Frank returned. Fortunately, he had managed to introduce Chi Bay as cook at the embassy house where he was allowed a small room and bath. So even before he had time for more than a shower and a change of clothing, I was there with him. Although he continued to be as reticent as usual about his duties in recent months, we embraced and for me all was in balance with his arms about me. For just a few days, he would be around Saigon reporting, clarifying, discussing, and meeting with others in and out of offices. Late at night, after singing in several clubs, I would join him in his room. All seemed normal—as normal as could be while Viet Nam was at war.

He explained to me, one afternoon, that the principal reason for his coming to Saigon involved reorganizing his work. All the Vietnamese with him had been supported by a civilian office, but now they were transferring entirely to special forces. Arrangements were already complete, and that night there would be a celebratory dinner at a restaurant between Saigon and Cho Lon. The next day everyone would disperse to various locations, but Frank promised two more days in Saigon with me. I thought the next day would be the best opportunity to tell him that I was pregnant with our child, conceived during his November visit. I anticipated our baby linking a perpetually shared future. I could not have known that that night would be our last together in Viet Nam.

The next morning, while we were still in bed, came a knocking on our bedroom door, and a voice announcing that one of his friends, Vann, needed to see him right away. The Vietnamese door knocker waited in a jeep while Frank clothed himself, kissed me, and promised to return as soon as possible. I feared otherwise, but in less than an hour he was back. The news he bore was grim. Douglas Ramsey, the person who introduced us about two and a half years before, had been captured the previous afternoon near Trung Lap northwest of Saigon. Frank, Vann, and two Vietnamese field operators would go there and try by one means or another to retrieve Doug. This would seem an act of madness to others, but it was one that I understood as dues paid within the brotherhood.

Three days passed, life in a painful vacuum for me; I could barely breathe. Then Frank appeared at my house, dirty, weary, looking more apparition than the man I loved. There were friends of my own, a painter and two journalists, in my living room. Frank offered no greeting, only took my hand and led me to the kitchen. He abruptly told me that it was not possible to continue dividing himself between me and the war. He would not return to Saigon and continue to share my life. There was no time for us, no space for me in his world. I was instantly paralyzed, fell to the floor, and cried out, weeping uncontrollably. Frank turned and was gone.

The air was sucked from my home. My mother rushed to raise me from the floor, but I could not speak. Frank had not allowed any opportunity for me to say a word, to engage with him, to express my feelings, to have a chance to show my understanding of his torment. He decided, entirely by himself, acting for himself, and then he was gone. And he would never know that I carried his son or daughter.

For a month, even several days more, I was barely alive. My mother cared for me as though I were an ill child again. I would not have minded dying. I staggered around our small house alternately crying and screaming. I ceased singing in Saigon clubs. Who, in my place, could have entertained others with happy songs and ballads? I was starving myself, miscarried, and sank ever deeper into depression. Only a sense of responsibility for family, my three children at school in Dalat, and the loving care of my mother kept me alive.

Otherwise, it would not have bothered me to die. I did not fear death. But slowly, very slowly, I stabilized and after several weeks, although thin and wan of face, resumed singing.

So, Frank had made his choice. He chose to go far from me, without allowing me any expression of my own feelings. Now I would strangle love, suppress memories, and look only to my own future. As he cared more for his friends in war, so now I would not care a bit for him.

About three months later, sometime in April, Frank unexpectedly reappeared in Dalat. I was spending time there with the children, recovering my spirits, reorienting my life. At midday I was with Ong Ngoai (my maternal grandfather) and a friend, working to improve our front-yard garden and decorative pond. Suddenly, and typically without notice, Frank was there. Awkwardly, barely smiling, he pointed to the Viet Nam Army truck that had brought him from Cam Ly airstrip to my house and said that he had brought a hot water heater with him for the family. Hot water heater! As he spoke, two soldiers dismounted from the rear of the truck and wrestled a large canister device to the ground at the side of our driveway.

Only a few weeks earlier I had miscarried our child. I now felt that I would rather see him boiled in hot water than accept any gift. We looked, with a sort of perplexed stare, his and mine, upon each other. Ong Ngoai took a few steps back and sideways to place himself behind me, as if out of a line of fire, and the friend who had been helping us smiled awkwardly and stepped aside, puzzled but aware of tension. Frank uncertainly remarked that he could see I was busy and paused as though waiting for my invitation to stay.

I would not so easily provide that, or any other expression of interest in what he might have wanted to say. So, shrugging, sensing my mood and glancing at the sky, he simply said, "Well, the plane is waiting for me at Cam Ly; good-bye then," and turning away, he moved to climb up and take a seat in the truck cab. The Vietnamese army driver, who with two other soldiers had been interested observers, also mounted and, switching on the ignition, drove away with Frank.

I staggered backward and was caught and steadied by my grandfather, exactly as he had sometimes done for me when I was a little girl in his Tra Vinh hamlet twenty years past. "Go, catch him," he whispered.

I ran toward the house. Our driver was absent, but I knew there was a spare set of keys in my room somewhere. It seemed to take forever to find them, and then when discovered and I was again outside, my car was even facing the wrong direction. While our dogs barked, I spun the car around, with engine stalling and then restarting and wheels spraying gravel, and I was on my way.

I knew that the truck in which Frank had left, an old army truck permanently parked at Cam Ly airstrip for military use, was slow, and that was good. But I was far to the rear and could not even see it. The road to Cam Ly went through Dalat town. I hoped they might have to stop for traffic or some other reason, any reason, but that driver was hurrying back to his station. While driving very fast on the road paralleling the Cam Ly stream, with the airstrip on the other side—almost, but not quite, there—I could already hear the distinctive ratcheting twin engines of an army Caribou winding up for takeoff.

I drove faster, even recklessly, and finally turned sharply onto the tarmac parking area. There was the truck, and there were the driver and two soldiers; but far down the runway and already lifting away was the plane taking Frank from me. I thought, but perhaps only imagined, the rear ramp was open. But even so, I could not see whether anyone stood looking back to the airfield. A few heartbeats, that was all, then just a speck in the sky, and finally, nothing.

My continued hurt and righteous anger had combined to distract and blind me. There may have been some chance for clarity, realignment, but on that afternoon when he reached out for me, I drew back until too late, and now Frank was gone again and I knew not where. My eyes blurred; my throat seemed obstructed as though I were choking. I felt incipient tears, but gritted my teeth and clenched my fists to control myself. I was justifiably angry, furious with Frank, and at the same time could not understand my emotional reaction.

"Two roads diverged in a wood, and long I stood," or something to that effect and mood, wrote an American poet. I stood long by that lonely runway, wishing, willing the noisy Caribou to return; but it did not, and after a long, long hour, I drove slowly home with a heavy, heavy heart.

CHAPTER 9

Adjustments

A rriving home after a futile wait at the Cam Ly airfield, leaving my car by the back entrance and entering through the kitchen, I found my family at the dinner table. Upon their seeing me, their conversation withered to anxious whispers. Denying them any opportunity for questions, I very quickly asked their allowance for some quiet time, all by myself, and so went directly to my room. I would have walked right through anyone who might have thought to slow me. Alone, I lay upon my bed, wrapped my arms around the long Vietnamese pillow, and allowed myself unwitnessed tears. I simply wanted to completely drain all emotion. Later, some other day, I could think about what had just happened. At the moment, I only wanted to staunch my bleeding heart.

However, I could not but wonder how close we might have been to bridging a wide chasm of misunderstanding. A matter of a minute or two, had he not been so quick to leave, or had my reaction not been slow, could have made a difference, but luck does not favor the indecisive. I sobbed without respite, and as I never have since. Hours later I woke, exhausted, but determined to make a new beginning. I would never again consider blaming myself. It was Frank who had been careless of our love. He was the one who walked away. I would bury, deep within, a bitter memory of his making the choice to break my heart, with no fair chance for me to speak, to maybe help him through a dark place and time. I would never see him again. Meanwhile, I had a duty to family, my children and my parents. I needed to preserve my sanity. I would move on.

I spent the next day completely focused on my children, deciding that the two boys best remain in Dalat to continue school with familiar teachers and classmates while I would bring my first child, daughter Le Thu, with me to attend school in Saigon. On the following morning, my mother and I shopped early for fresh Dalat vegetables and strawberries, then we were on our way back to Saigon, a journey of six hours by road.

I resumed a full schedule of nightclub singing, with one significant difference. The previous occasional appearance of Frank, or one of his friends, and my greetings and conversations with them, made clear to regular club and restaurant attendees that I was already committed, promised by myself to another, and so was absolutely unobtainable. Now I was at risk of embarrassment by importunate customers. Many followed me from one venue to the next. And, abandoned by one American—I am sorry to confess—I felt something like hatred for all others. This period of my life was unmistakably acidic. My only relief was that my good friend Kim Chi, who had left Nha Trang to stay with me, counseled patience, temperate behavior, and a renewed focus on my career.

So, 1966 was an awfully painful, discouraging year for me, and no different for my country. Ambitious self-promoted general officers, passing stars among themselves as would children, during the previous year jostled for the position of new national leader in replacement of Nguyen Khanh, he who had replaced Duong Van Minh ... who had previously led the conspiracy to murder President Diem. Now, a sort of military council organized around the prime minister and air force general Nguyen Cao Ky, with some degree of oversight by army general Nguyen Van Thieu, decided to rid themselves of persistently critical general Nguyen Chanh Thi, who commanded in the Hue–Danang region. Unexpectedly, the dismissal was so unpopular that people, especially Buddhists, organized demonstrations, and some military units in Hue and Danang expressed strong disapproval. We avoided an actual civil war, but the regional resistance was only suppressed with extreme loss of life, and General Thi was sent off to something like "medical leave" exile. Americans seemed to me more complicit, perhaps even the determinators, of all that transpired in my country.

In Saigon, friends told me, there were two or three streets where it was best that a Vietnamese woman avoid walking alone, even by day. And in my own entertainer's life, I witnessed the American bluster and presumption of privilege every evening. Nightclub audiences were almost entirely American, and many acted as though being saviors of our country should be a license for outlandish behavior. They called to women and sometimes would even grab one by the arm as though they believed we were a country of prostitutes. On an evening in Ma Ca Ban, after I finished my performance of four songs, thanked the audience, and began walking to the door, a man fondled my buttock while I passed his table. Enraged, I snatched a glass ashtray from that table and smashed it into his face. He stumbled backward and I threw the ashtray but, missing him, broke the window fronting the boulevard. That terrible man fled, embarrassed and probably cut up quite a bit. The manager-owner charged me for his plate-glass window. I did not mind, because the incident cemented my reputation for being untouchable.

One day, in early summer 1966, Chi Bay came to see me. She thought I should know that Frank had returned, ill, to Saigon. She had debated whether it was best to tell me or let the past stay in the past. Finally, she thought, if I were to learn from another person that my lost love had reappeared but that she had not told me, perhaps I would consider her less a friend. I embraced Chi Bay and told her that I would rather be informed than surprised. She said

Frank had been in a military hospital on Hai Ba Trung Street for a few days but was now in his old room at the embassy house where she still worked. I asked how he seemed, emphasizing that I meant only to ask after his health. I had no other interest and told her that I was sure it would be best for both him and me not to visit. Chi Bay looked at me a bit doubtfully but nodded and left.

Several days passed. I, not caring for Frank any longer and having cured myself of all that, would not deign to visit. But eventually, after some time convincing myself of a complete lack of concern, I decided to be a better person than he and so go as an old friend to enquire about his condition. But while I had been marking time and persuading myself of my own better nature—better than his—all changed once more. I found that he was gone somewhere far away again. Chi Bay confirmed that she had not told him about meeting with me. He recovered some strength and only two days earlier packed everything, which was not much at all, in a big military bag and an old sort of backpack and went away in a jeep with a driver. Gone, gone, and gone. I was relieved, and I was sad, just a bit. But knew now there was no impediment to taking my own road, unencumbered by heavy memories.

Entirely separately—unconnected to foregone opportunity for reconnection, and with no repetition of a thrown ashtray—I continued to look on Americans with some bitterness. Why were there now so many in Saigon? Why did they appear so assured of their own superiority? Why did they behave so rudely? And just as important, why were they not far from Saigon in battle? What could all these foreigners be doing in Saigon? Who decided as to those who would fight and those who could play? An old question, and one, in truth, that could be asked of many Vietnamese, too.

There was one positive, beneficial consequence of the spring 1966 political turmoil. As a means of smoothing the roiling political waters, the military leaders promised elections for a constituent assembly tasked to write a constitution. When the new document, in replacement of that suspended by the 1963 murder of President Diem, was complete, it was debated by the military leadership and, with the exception of striking the election of province governors, was accepted, with its implementation scheduled for the following year.

As an entertainer, singer of tragic love songs as I was, my strong interest in what happened in my country was still constant. I was tempted to feel that we had "turned a corner" from the 1965 near-collapse to the late-1966 commitment for a constitutional, responsive, and responsible government.

Saigon was exhibiting the consequences of being a capital in the midst of war. Refugees, country people fleeing artillery and air-strikes as much as communist depredation, relocated to city streets, alleys, and a few previously empty tracts of urban land. Tents, then shacks, at first temporary but later permanent, spread wherever tolerated. Rents increased, and not just because of the growing number of Americans and their supporting allies but also because relatively well-to-do rural families sought city safety. For the first time there was visible air pollution because of the almost constant military truck traffic. Saigon was the hub for highway spokes moving large numbers of soldiers and supplies from one point to another. Some of our beautiful trees were cut down to widen streets so that traffic could move easily, albeit still slowly.

Despite difficulties, restaurants were crowded again, and shops were thronged with Vietnamese. They were feeling secure for the moment and, not without reason, believed that no matter the complications, prospects seemed to be improving for some of us. My continued singing produced income sufficient for all the family needs, but my two boys, with Mother and Father, were still living in the mountains. Every month I returned to Dalat for two or three days, usually by road, and except for some deteriorating Highway 20 road surfaces, we noticed little change. Boulder-upon-boulder formations placed during the Paleolithic still rested at Dinh Quan, untouched by modern-man war. Tea and coffee plantations around Blao and Djirling in Lam Dong Province appeared quiet.

Unlike many other province capitals, Dalat was escaping almost all war strain. One had to look hard to find people who might be refugees from war in the surrounding provinces. I thought at the time it was because Dalat and adjacent districts were relatively low priority for both sides, but another grim possibility was that the local government might be accommodating in some way in order to preserve a Dalat atmosphere for the privileged. Could it also have been that the communists had their own interests to protect in that city?

I made myself ignore the past, live in the present, and always look to the future: to forget the illusion of love and think only of my children. My resolve was tested only once, just a few months later in spring 1967. I was with faithful Kim Chi, walking up Tu Do Street toward a favorite bookstore. Passing what would become the National Assembly Building, we saw Frank and a friend coming toward us, so close that an encounter could not be avoided. Quickly, taking the initiative, I called out with false cheerfulness, "Here . . . it seems to be Frank Scotton, but it cannot be! He never comes to Saigon!"

Frank looked like a thief caught in the act, but then he spoke, in a voice so low that Kim Chi and I needed to strain forward, telling us that he was there to accompany his friend, who just that week had tested positive for tuberculosis and so must leave Viet Nam. His friend, whom I remembered from two years past, tall and lanky like a screen cowboy, sadly nodded and confirmed that he had asked Frank to come to Saigon to make the promise that when he was again declared medically fit, Frank would arrange orders for his return to Viet Nam. So, feeling a little embarrassed, having thought I had unmasked my former love but instead finding that he was simply in the company of another foolish romantic warrior, I nodded and walked away with Kim Chi.

She nudged me in my right arm with her left elbow and advised me, "Turn around, go back, just once, just this time. Tell him that you miss him, wish him well, and then see what will happen." I glared at her and responded that we were both, Frank and I, long past romance and sentimental gestures. It should instead be he, the one who had stabbed my heart, seeking reconnection, and not for me to appear so needy for him. So, just as Longfellow's ships at sea, we slowly passed away from each other that spring on a Saigon city street.

Election campaigning in mid-1967 was exciting, not just because we Vietnamese had been governed non-democratically for so many years, but also because many of us believed there was a chance for significant change. On the American side, the autocratic Cabot Lodge, clueless aristocrat, promoter of the 1963 coup and 1966 cheerleader for Danang suppression instead of compromise, was finally gone for good. His replacement, Ellsworth Bunker, no less the aristocrat, seemed more inclined to at least occasionally listen to a Vietnamese voice.

The fall 1967 elections had some peculiarities. There was, of course, a military candidate for president, General Nguyen Van Thieu, with his restive colleague General Nguyen Cao Ky harnessed for vice president, but there were also civilian candidates, although the latter were hobbled by lack of resources. Representatives for a "lower house" congress could run as individuals, while would-be senators had to be one name on a "ticket" of ten persons. A very respectable acquaintance on one of the senate tickets asked me to participate in campaigning. But there were others on the same ticket that I thought should not have presumed to seek office. And, very much according to Vietnamese cultural form, I thought it best to abstain from any public endorsement.

Ours is a family-centered society. The generally positive feature of this characteristic is the willingness to sacrifice for family. The less positive, more problematic, aspect is a tendency to refrain from even a small risk of embarrassment or injury to family, so sometimes there is a reluctance to align with a different, especially minority, point of view. And, even more negatively, calculating the benefits to family is the basis, I think, for rationalizing the frequent abuse of position, a common form of corruption: "I do it for the family, not for myself."

Month after month, when not in Dalat to reconnect with my children, even though sometimes agonizing over my lost relationship with a man who I had thought would share a long life with me, I was singing, singing, singing. I do love music, but music as extended labor—too many venues, too many hours every night—was a consequence of my being the sole provider for not just my immediate family but also members of the extended family. Some, like the father of my mother who had sheltered us in Tra Vinh more than twenty years earlier, were loved so deeply that failure to provide small amounts of money was unimaginable. Others, like the uncle who drove me from venue to venue, obviously needed payment for the service provided; had he not been helping me, someone else would have to be hired, someone perhaps less responsible. But there were also a few distant relatives, maybe more than a few, who would pester my mother for small sums, and she felt obligated to accede to them.

I don't think anyone in the family understood the emotional and real physical stress that brought me to absolute collapse in November 1967. I was experiencing pain in and around my vocal cords, deep within my throat. Swallowing throat lozenges and consuming smooth fruit drinks (banana and durian) no longer sufficed to relieve the discomfort. My performances were affected, and my morale sank. I sought medical evaluation and reluctantly accepted a diagnosis that indicated surgery would be advisable. Today, robotic and laser procedures have advanced to the point that what was then necessary for me is now considered a minor procedure. But fifty years ago, the removal of polyps on vocal cords did not seem at all minor. I was nervous and fearful, because if injury were permanent, or the treatment unsuccessful, our family would financially collapse.

My friend Kim Chi, a constant stalwart emotional supporter, sat by my bed and told funny stories that kept me smiling when it was still difficult to speak. Two of the military academy instructors with whom I was acquainted came to visit and suggested that when freed from the hospital, I ought to spend a few weeks in Dalat to recuperate with my family in the clean air. Their advice readily became my intention.

I worried about the medical fees and the continuing need to meet family expenses. Another visitor provided assistance that I still remember with deep appreciation. Ralf Jonson had often attended nightclubs where I sang. He was always friendly without presuming that I could be his playmate. Later I met him again as a friend of Frank. Now he visited my hospital room, and, after other visitors departed, insisted that I accept a thick envelope stuffed with money to cover the hospital bills. I protested. He explained that the gift was not from him alone: Others who missed my singing had also contributed, with no expectation except hope that I recover as soon as possible. Whether this generous act was his own doing or truly on behalf of a few others, I shed some tears of gratitude.

About three weeks later I was, with my indispensable driver, able to make the several hours' drive to Dalat while Kim Chi remained in Saigon. It was mid-December and, nestled in the mountains, Dalat was naturally cool by day and cold at night. But there was another kind of noticeable chill too. One week earlier, a government reconnaissance force, investigating an overrun outpost to the south, was ambushed. The senior American advisor, other Americans, and many Vietnamese soldiers, were killed. This was an unprecedented show of force by communists in the Dalat area. I was concerned but not extraordinarily alarmed because we were eventually bound to get a taste of what every other part of Viet Nam had endured.

By early January 1968, my recovery seemed complete, and I was singing normally, without strain, in and around our mountain home. It had been wondrous to have Christmas with the family in Dalat. All seemed well until, one evening a few days before my return to Saigon, Father noticed several men in dark clothing moving toward town from within the ravine behind our property. We checked all the door locks and made sure every interior window shutter was secure. The next morning, we found that our dogs had been poisoned.

I was all for the entire family immediately driving to Saigon. But Father and Mother thought my reaction extreme. This was Dalat! So, I kept to my schedule and, on the day planned, after hugging and kissing the children in farewell, I was on my way back to Saigon. I was definitely worried, though, because the town that I had thought inviolate seemed perhaps not as snugly and smugly untouched by war as before. Moreover, our immediate neighborhood included a property of the French consulate, and another leased to house a small American military detachment.

Back in Saigon, and with Kim Chi helping me, I prepared my schedule for the approaching Lunar New Year round of nightclub performances and parties. Preliminary festivities began a few days in advance, and I was much in demand both for singing at special sponsored celebrations and for a regular schedule of nightclubs. When the actual New Year's Eve was way past midnight, my schedule for that day was completed! The fatigue was so overwhelming that I suggested to Kim Chi and our driver that we ride around the city and watch neighborhood celebrations before arriving home. A new year was beginning, Year of the Monkey, said to be of mischievous nature.

How cruelly that folk belief proved true. Just as we were turning into the long dirt driveway to our house off Truong Minh Giang, we saw—absurdly, obscenely, suspended from an electric power pole—the body of a neighbor, hanging by his leg. I had shocking evidence before my eyes that not all the sounds heard that evening stemmed from snapping firecrackers.

The communist attacks—Tet, 1968—were countrywide. There may have been an untouched province, but I do not know of it. My mother spoke with me by phone, amazingly still working, to report that my boys in Dalat were safe, and their school was untouched, but communist soldiers penetrated the market square and roamed freely through town for two days before, like a monsoon flooding, finally receding. Kim Chi, whose family was originally from Hue, learned from friends that her hometown was taken over by the communists, and American soldiers were fighting them in the streets while our Vietnamese soldiers held their positions within the citadel fortress.

Saigon was paralyzed. Restaurants and nightclubs closed. Streets were deserted, as everyone stayed home to bar entry and protect their families. Americans generally remained in their rented houses and military quarters unless engaged in operations to drive communist forces from the city. The Hanoi offensive planners and coordinators may have expected, or simply told their combatants for morale purposes, that their Tet Offensive would spark a general uprising against the Republic and our American ally, but nothing like that occurred in any province. However, as a cautionary tale for our government, the communist offensive depended to a great extent on prepositioning assault units and supplies. Many Vietnamese in hamlets adjacent to our capital, in provincial towns and bases, would have observed that activity, and the communists were not generally betrayed. So, it seemed proven that too many citizens were still inconstant fence-sitters.

The fear and paralytic atmosphere enveloping Saigon caused restaurants and nightclubs to close doors and turn out lights. The simultaneous rising prices of food staples, due to the greater risk on principal roads from provinces, sharply increased the real cost of living. In a matter of days, the situation became desperate, as many of the extended family members, relatives of Mother and Father, were accustomed to drawing sustenance from my income; we were all drawn down to the last piaster. I was distraught at not having a way to maintain the welfare of those dependent on me.

Just then, and to a great surprise as much as a relief, a few Americans who had often followed me from venue to venue, even those who sometimes behaved in an insulting manner and occasionally followed me home and against whom my driver always locked the driveway gate as soon as we were within, now with almost bashful manner brought boxes of PX food to our gate, rang the bell, and with a brief wave departed. Strange, our human nature: sometimes at its worst, and sometimes surprisingly much better.

We shared everything with neighbors, not only because the American generosity was too much for our own family but also because sharing was the politic and prudent step required to avoid incurring jealousy that could spark resentment. Even with that assistance, with food delivered right to our door, I was still short on the income necessary for school fees, money to meet parental needs, and for paying our driver and home assistance help.

Just when it appeared necessary to borrow funds at outrageous interest, another pest from the past stepped forward and offered me a job at "Radio Freedom," the American-funded and -managed station for broadcasting Viet Nam news, all decidedly anti-communist. Michael Brown, previously one of those nightclub patrons who would fall over himself for a smile, hired me for on-the-air announcing and occasional commentary. Now he could make, but from behind studio glass, moon faces all day. I did not care. He stepped up to help, and my family benefited.

Several weeks later, when municipal security was much improved and reinforced by checkpoints and an extended curfew, Saigon revived, with reopened highways bringing produce to the markets again. Restaurants, then nightclubs, quickly reopened. One evening Ralf Jonson, proven good friend, with another American accompanying asked to sit with me at a side table where singers customarily waited their turn to perform. He rather urgently said with some intensity that I ought to think seriously about finding a way to move my family out of Viet Nam. I countered, "Why now? Why are you so sure? Our situation has improved. Communists are already retreating from cities and towns!"

He responded that, having seen what occurred in Hue, where communists killed hundreds of captives before withdrawing, and considering the probability that the retreat was not permanent, he expected that people like me would not be gently, or even fairly, treated if taken prisoner. Moreover, he continued, my parents and children would suffer because of their relationship with me. With a smile, Ralf suggested there would be a long line of men proposing marriage and a new home abroad, but I should make sure they understood that parents and children would comprise an essential part of the package. Ralf rose, patted me on the shoulder, turned and was gone. We did not meet again. Decades later, I learned that he married a young woman who had worked for the American embassy. I believe he was surely as responsible a husband as he was a friend for many others.

I did not feel ready to think about leaving my country. I was reluctant to assume the burden borne by my mother more than twenty years earlier when she organized the family escape from Saigon to the Tra Vinh sanctuary. The observation that more than a few men were ready to provide me with a lifeline, a way out and away from war, was correct. But Ralf was also wise in advising me to be wary. An older, senior officer, connected with one of those war-profiting American contractors supporting the vast enterprise of building infrastructure for ports and warehousing, roads, airfields, and communications, confided to me that his wife was very ill and could not live long. He offered to bring me to Hong Kong, house me luxuriously, provide more money "than I could spend," and marry me when circumstances would allow. But his lack of interest in my family, the mean description of his wife, and the descriptive terms of enrichment rather than endearment, caused me to smell a rat.

A young American named John was ardent and, I thought, sincere. He promised to bring my children with me to America and care for them with something of the love that he felt for me. But although he expressed an equivalent concern for my mother and father, I was not entirely convinced. And I could no more chance leaving them behind than they would have risked separating from me in 1945. So at least temporarily I shelved that offer, saying that we both could think about it, while he returned home to America.

Meanwhile, some Chinese businessmen had initiated an apparently successful venture based on quail eggs. Two of them proposed to provide me with setting quail hens and promised to purchase eggs from me for resale to restaurants. Our house along the creek by Truong Minh Giang was not large, but the whole family could pitch in to help. An American who was one of those who followed me from club to club pledged to obtain an incubator so that eggs would hatch to provide even more quail, therefore eventually increasing eggs exponentially. Soon we had so many quail putting out eggs, and generationally making more quail for even more eggs, that Mother and Kim Chi complained we were being smothered by quail feathers and quail poop. We made so much money from this quail venture that Mother was bundling piasters in old rice bags and hiding them in a closet.

I gave some of the quail to women in the neighborhood and decided to quit messing with feathers and eggs by placing the accumulated proceeds in a business less "foul." Only a few weeks later, as it had with tulips long ago in Europe, the market price of quail and eggs began to drop due to excess supply. I released the remaining birds, but they kept returning home until over time the few survivors became table fare for our family and neighbors.

I opened a small business downtown by applying quail egg proceeds combined with a loan to open Trung Tam Thau Bang Kim Vui (Kim Vui Recording Center) in rented premises. We provided recording, duplication, and music printing services. An associated enterprise allowed customers to make photocopies and sold printer paper and imported copy machines. I believed that building a dependable non-feathered source of income would stabilize our family finances.

Because of my recognizable face, some "sidewalk people," most lacking a regular address and a roof, began to cluster near the doorway. At first, I provided them with small amounts of money for food, asking only that they allow space for customers to enter our business. Most of them were elderly women. Remembering how kindly old neighborhood women had befriended me when I was young, and all those who had helped when my father had forced me from home while first pregnant, I could not deny them considerate attention and help. When one of those ladies died, my mother and I furnished the burial money. I was not so angelic as it might have appeared, but I was there. Seeing someone in need, you can either help or turn away. I could not turn away.

CHAPTER 10

Adrift

U nexpectedly, at the beginning of summer 1968, an international entertainment company, in the person of a visiting representative, approached me one night after my performance at the Hotel Majestic and asked if I would consider joining an Asian talent ensemble for a special performance in Las Vegas. I was immediately interested, willing but simultaneously apprehensive. Women traveling on their own, among strangers—even though many of the latter may also be women—need take to care. My best friend Kim Chi and my mother cautiously endorsed travel with the troupe, thinking that it could be an antidote to my continuing unhappiness. The passport and visa issues were expeditious because the project had government approval. After just a few days, which passed like a fast-forwarding video, we few were off by way of Tokyo to America!

I knew that another young Vietnamese singer, Bach Yen, she of sweet voice and modest temperament and a southerner like me, had traveled to the United States from France a few years earlier. She had performed in Las Vegas, on stage and television; but Bach Yen was still abroad somewhere in France or perhaps even still in America. Lacking the opportunity to speak with her, I did not know what to expect; therefore Las Vegas, even fifty years ago, was a shocking desert apparition.

My first exposure to this city was all about bright lights: the twinkling, the flashing, the intensity of color. The next impact on this inexperienced traveler was my feeling of being surrounded, almost overwhelmed, by crowds, indeed swarms, of people—on the sidewalk, in and around and within pleasure palaces, everyone moving frantically, like ants running on ant trails to and fro. Other than those at card and dice tables, and people concentrating on pulling the arms of game machines, everyone else was in perpetual motion. My third insistent impression was that Las Vegas was steeped in the perfume of sex for money. There were women within and without those gambling palaces who were obviously available for casual encounters. I could not even begin to imagine what might be practiced in darker, less public, places. Thinking of my childhood in a Saigon–Cho Lon district wherein a criminal enterprise, the Binh Xuyen, held license for policing while simultaneously trafficking in gambling, opium, and women, I thought that those Vietnamese gangsters of old would be stunned by the scale of Las Vegas businesses legitimately profiting from temptations attendant to human frailty.

Our limited performance was part of a package arranged within a large hotel and entertainment establishment that awed me. There may have been places in Las Vegas more complex and impressive fifty years ago, but I did not see them. Pulling up memories of long ago, I remember the hotel complex appearing very much like a beehive, with constant motion and an incessant buzz that may have been a form of surround sound but could have simply been the sonic vibration of excited paying guests. I vaguely remember a glass ceiling and how it frightened me to think that it could fall, dangerously shattering, if the workmanship was flawed or if shaken by an earthquake vibration. The impression was one of definite glitter, but with sharp edges. Unavoidably, I kept thinking of a Binh Xuyen gangster simile.

I had the feeling that this Las Vegas project was in the nature of a trial balloon, a test of audience reaction. My own performance, including an American soldier favorite, "Love is a Many-Splendored Thing," was so welcomed by the audience standing and cheering that I was alarmed, as I had been once when much younger, mistaking the noise for disapproval. An offered explanation soothed me and so, relaxed, I sang an encore.

The Count Basie band was playing in Las Vegas at the same time. Our troupe manager told me that Basie had heard me sing and could offer an engagement with his ensemble, predicated on my switching from popular songs to jazz. I was not sure that change would be possible for me, and any contract would have to be an amended extension of the one already signed for bringing me with others to America. He explained that an extension procedure would be necessary to meet passport and visa requirements. I had not known of Count Basie's reputation, so insular was I at home in Saigon; but as explained to me, the chance to work with his band was like hitting a Las Vegas multi-machine jackpot. I asked for a copy of the draft contract, as it would be amended, so that I could telephone my mother. In wanting to speak with her, I was not just being careful; in truth I was entirely bewildered, not knowing what the best but also prudent step would be. I could not distinguish between opportunity and a possibly exploitable situation.

The telephone connection was difficult, and my limited English-language ability was overwhelmed by the convoluted contract text; but my mother helped me make a decision. The amended contract seemed to provide greater financial benefit for the original troupe manager than for me. An actual link to Mr. Basie seemed vague and tenuous, and one way or another I could have been too easily disposable, adrift in a strange land wherein I barely spoke the language and had no protector. My mother feared that accepting that contract would be too much like signing my life away. She suggested that I first take a month or so to see something of America, while thinking about whether or not I would feel comfortable in a strange land. I should then return to Viet Nam and make a decision.

There was the young man, John, who had proposed marriage before he left Viet Nam. My response had been that we both needed to think carefully rather than acting in haste. Now it occurred to me that he would be a reliable person with whom something of America could be seen and understood.

John accepted my telephone call and, still an ardent suitor, said that since I was already in America, he wanted to invite me for a visit with his family in Key West where I could stay with his mother while we got reacquainted. But first, he suggested, we should meet in Washington, DC, because this would be a great chance to see the capital of America. That was an amazing suggestion, an idea that had not occurred to me. I had a good friend in Virginia; staying with her would be a check against the implication of an immediate physical relationship with John. So, with no regret and some actual feeling of relief, I departed Las Vegas, home of sanctioned licentious behavior, on a flight to Washington, DC, the seat of government for the greatest power of our time.

I had already contacted Lang Miller, former owner of the Kon Tiki nightclub in Saigon and sister to Tran Thi Hoa, who many years before frequently accompanied me while moving from one singing engagement to another, all while I had suffered in an abusive marriage. I always tried to hide the physical and emotional damage, but Hoa had held my hand and cried for me. I trusted her, and so would trust her sister Lang who had married an American and moved to Virginia.

Lang met me on my arrival at National Airport. On a cold but sunny day, our approach over the Potomac River allowed this naive international traveler the visual appreciation of grand buildings, predominantly white stone, spread around an extensive well-treed grassy parkland north of the wide river. I thought of Washington, the seat of the American elected government, as an imperial city, because, like Rome or London in centuries past, measured (poorly or not) policies and decisions made here would be accepted and implemented by dependent, or semi-dependent, nations acquiescing to Washington's primacy.

We Vietnamese were inescapably familiar with the Chinese imperial practice of previous centuries; fearing future repetition, we were not slow to recognize a similar pattern, no matter how disguised or well-intentioned, practiced by America. Please do not assume my analytical comparison is unfounded. The American "green light" authorizing a 1963 military coup resulting in the murder of President Diem is a painful, all-too-clear illustration, and there are definitely others, like the decision particulars of the 1965 deployment of entire American Army and Marine divisions and, beginning in 1968, the now-known details of secret American negotiations in Paris for ending hostilities in my country.

My immediate concerns that summer were much more personal. John stayed in a hotel while I was a guest of Lang and her husband. We included John in all our daily and evening activities. Our schedule was purely touristic but did include one late afternoon/early evening reception, suggested by Lang but hosted by Ambassador Bui Diem and his wife. Bui Diem had been appointed by President Thieu to represent the Republic of Viet Nam. He was about fifteen years older than I, and he was a northerner of privileged family birth, who previously had been a successful publisher in Saigon. He was, in the context of the social occasion that day, both impressive by his comportment and very hospitable. Perhaps he would not remember me fifty years later, but I do recall that he seemed tired, perhaps even a bit mournful. It is so very difficult representing a dependent nation in an imperial capital, whether Rome of ancient history or benevolent Washington on the Potomac.

Before departing Washington, we visited Arlington National Cemetery and the grave of President John Kennedy. This is a hallowed place, with somber rows of buried men and women who served America to their final breath. I thought of the awful symmetry represented by President Diem of my country and American President Kennedy being murdered within a few weeks of each other. And I could not refrain from thinking of Frank's father interred in a similar American military cemetery somewhere in Europe.

A few days later, John and I left for Key West. Lifting away from National Airport, I had no premonition, even remotely, that several years later I would be living and working in the Washington area.

Key West, our destination, dangles sort of southward off Florida, or at least on a map appears so. John's mother, whose name I recall as Olga, kindly, even enthusiastically, greeted me at her door. The genuinely warm welcome seemed to suggest that she would care for me as if I were her special guest. That foreclosed any potentially awkward speculation as to where I might find a bed if having to stay in John's own house.

We enjoyed touring the shops, visited another small island by boat, and took a trip to Miami; although conversing around and around the subject for a few days, John and I could not arrive at a mutually comfortable decision concerning marriage. He had previously proposed in Saigon and pursued me to Dalat, all at a time when I thought we barely knew, much less understood, each other. I did feel comfortable with John, as a friend, and I enjoyed every Key West day, thinking to myself that someday Viet Nam coastal islands, just as attractively situated, could also be tourist destinations.

John had a twin brother, and when the brother visited, the two of them delighted in playing tricks with me at mealtime, dressing alike and making me guess which one was John. That game, amusing at first, but then repetitious, finally seemed a bit distressing to me because their amusement derived from my discomfort.

So, all things considered, the Key West renewed marriage proposal did not feel correct for me. I returned home to Viet Nam. After a few months, I received a letter from John with news that he had entered into a relationship with a nurse in Florida and would soon marry her, but would never (he wrote) forget me. And you will have seen, by these pages, that I also recall him and his mother's kindness.

It was simply wonderful to be home in Viet Nam again. I did not question whether I had been too picky when thinking about an American escape route; in any case, the southern Viet Nam in late 1968 seemed to be stabilizing. The attacking communist units had suffered grievous losses. The previous Tet offensive panic in Saigon evaporated. There were a few terrorist attacks—a deadly bomb placed in the Tu Do nightclub, for example—but many believed that sort of activity was actually an indicator of communist desperation.

Negotiations in Paris were still being conducted for the purpose of stopping conflict between South and North Viet Nam. Our American ally was the principal negotiator for our side. The commitment of American lives and resources had been so great that we Vietnamese believed the United States was still determined to guarantee an independent South. With very few exceptions, most of my friends absolutely trusted America. So rather than further pondering escape to a safe foreign sanctuary, I turned my attention once again to establishing a financially secure future for my family—children and parents—in the Republic of Viet Nam.

When departing for travel to America, I had entrusted the management and security of the recording and printing business, into which all quail egg money had been invested, to my ex-husband, Luong, from whom I had obtained a divorce more than three years earlier. I felt that even though he had abused me and destroyed our marriage, by being the father of our sons Bao and Khai he could be trusted, at least on their behalf, to do what was right. But, with financial temptation in hand, he was unable to control himself, and slowly siphoned off money for alcohol-fueled festivities and gambling with friends. When skimming profits became insufficient, he began to sell some of the stocked photo and print paper and finally even the very machines on which our business depended. I had hoped that my father and mother would be some brake on potential malfeasance. Now I realized, too late, that there had been one gaping hole in that safety net. My father was a probable, maybe even willing, beneficiary of Luong's misbehavior and theft, while as usual Mother avoided confronting Father.

My trying to calculate what might be done to cover our losses, consider correctives, and seek alternative ventures was not at all helped by the distracting reappearance of Frank. I was wakened on a late 1968 December morning by friend Kim Chi pulling on my pillow and telling me, "He is back, and downstairs waiting for you."

"Who?"

"Frank!"

"Tell him to go away!"

But Kim Chi responded that the visitor was my problem. "You should have told him long ago to stay or go," she said, but instead seemed to allow disappearing and reappearing. "And," she continued, "don't think that you can hide up here. He has a jeep in the driveway, and we can't go anywhere until you settle with him."

So not bothering to dress nicely for the visitor who had once been loved with all my heart, I descended the steps a few minutes later. Kim Chi disappeared into the kitchen, evading any involvement and probably wanting to avoid even witnessing what would be a very awkward encounter.

Frank was standing tall, and I took the chair furthest from where he stood. He asked whether I had time to talk. He appeared self-assured, as always, but was soliciting an opinion, as though my response might be determinative for him. Oh, if only we had approached each other that considerately some years past. But it was already late, for me, for him, and so for us. This was my response, my message for him.

"If you had spoken with me as you do now, been really open, ready to share feelings, whatever they may have been, those days almost three years ago, I would have wholeheartedly chosen a life with you, only you. But you never had time for talking with me, or maybe you did not know how. You just made the big decision by yourself, for yourself, without giving me, without giving us, a chance. Now you would like to know if I have time for talking! But I know that really means you want to explain your romantic attachment to war in my country. Like a ghost from Dalat in times past, you appear, disappear, and reappear. You may be confused, but you cannot confuse me, not even a little. Oh no, no more. Go back with your friends, those who think like you, the ones you chose to live with far out in woods and hamlets, rather than save even a little time for me. Yes, you made that choice, too long ago. It was always about you choosing, not me. But today I am the one to choose, and I decide for myself, not for you. You should leave. Never think of me again. Just go."

My lean blue-green-eyed lost love nodded, as though my words were just what he had anticipated, and he quietly moved toward the door. Then he paused, turned back slightly, and replied, "Not so simple as you say, as you think. I will always remember you, Kim Vui."

He took a few strides, then was in the jeep, backing away upward along the driveway, and so because he was looking rearward over his shoulder, he did not see me cry. But I could not contain my tears; too often, in the years that followed, I recalled that moment. I was really crying for both of us, because we should never have parted.

Fortunately for my emotional stability, in a few weeks I began working on two films that featured me as a principal actress. Both of them, *Cui Mat* (Downcast) and *Thuong Han* (Bitter Love) conveyed definite anti-communist themes. *Cui Mat* portrayed former communist adherents returning to the Saigon government side of the conflict through the *chieu hoi* (returnee) program that partially echoed the civic action projects that engaged me more than ten years earlier. My role in *Thuong Han* was that of a tough woman captain of the communist military who, wounded and captured by Republic of Viet Nam soldiers, was respectfully treated and saved

A pensive moment, following the break from the man loved and lost.

from death by blood transfusions provided by the very army against which she had been fighting. Within that cinematic story, a brave Vietnamese woman abandoned communism! Both films required

A popular film, *Cui Mat* (Downcast), within which I was supported by others that included former Viet Cong.

arduous physical effort because I never used a double and there were storyline requirements of carrying heavy weapons. In one scene (with multiple takes) I submerged myself in a river to attach a facsimile explosive charge to a bridge while warding off an unscripted snake!

For reasons obvious to readers, after 1975—when the communist party, owing to their military offensive of that year, seized control of our South Viet Nam—all copies of those films were destroyed, and I doubt that even one could be located today. However, in 1969 that time was still six years in the future, when much more would be at risk for all Vietnamese. How the communists might react to my films was never a concern for me. It mattered most, and especially for my family, that by those two films providing some immediate income we could revive our small printing and recording business.

The mirage of American sanctuary faded, in part because the necessity appeared less critical more than one year after the failed

Another popular film, *Thuong Han* (Bitter Love), in which I took the part of a wounded communist officer.

communist Tet Offensive, and also because I concluded it might not be possible to acquire a lifeline that would include parents as well as children. I sought diversion from constant singing performances by riding horses near the old Saigon racetrack and resuming my practice of archery. (And yes, sometimes I did picture the image of Frank on the target face!) I declined invitations to join the moneyed Cercle Sportif club in central Saigon because I thought it a neocolonial hangout for, and facilitator of, licentious liaison. The horse riders encountered at Hippique were more serious, not romantically intentioned, and I found peace there.

When I once more encountered Frank several months later, he was so very fortunate that my bow and arrows were not with me! I was driving on Le Van Duyet from downtown, a roundabout way toward my home, and then there he was, striding along in a purposeful way. I could not overcome the impulse to pull over, slightly ahead of his path, and emerge from the car to hail that haunt of my day and night dreams. He paused and then stopped in the shade of a tree alongside the road. I joined him there. He was, as he told me that afternoon, on his way to a liaison office much further up Le Van Duyet—a long walk, he said, but a good walk.

I asked where he had been those past several months since we last spoke. "In Taiwan," he replied, "sometimes back to Viet Nam, but very soon going somewhere else for a year or so. But not really far away, and I will often be back to Viet Nam when required."

It was the usual vague acknowledgment of his going somewhere but then having someone call him back, although it was never clear who that would be or what he might be doing if he returned. We were both quiet then. Our shared past was receding, like an outgoing tide on flat sand, draining away from the beach, all of a sudden too quickly.

What was left for either of us to say? I could only ask, not to prolong, but with some real curiosity, "How far from Viet Nam will you be?"

He responded, saying, "in Borneo by way of Singapore," then stunned me by adding in a rather disjointed way that he would soon marry—a young woman met in Taiwan who had just delivered a son.

I felt my heart pound, and my blood seemed to drain away along every vein, straight to my feet. I may have reeled. I wanted to scream, but did not, in a mix of anger and hurt: "A son! What about the child I carried that was yours? The child that I lost because you wandered off to deeper war with no thought, not even a bit of consideration, for me?"

Instead of that most honest reaction, I lied and countered, "Oh, I also will soon marry, an American engineer here in Saigon on contract." That may have fooled him, even while it soothed me not at all. My hasty response was a twist of reality, and even as a small act of self-consolation it was a sparse balm on my wounds, definitely not curative. But as he nodded, digesting the falsehood, I thought to myself, "Well, I probably will have to marry someone, someday, and of all the American contractors around Saigon there is more than one hopeful candidate."

For a moment or two, or three, we stood right there, oblivious to all around. I could have offered him a ride and we might have spoken further, but he had already burned that possibility by having told me that it was "a good walk." I did not want to hear that cool dismissal, if dismissal it was, again.

I asked whether he had any news of Douglas Ramsey, the friend who had introduced us six years earlier in Dalat and whose capture and long disappearance seemed to have morphed Frank from lover to grim love lost. His look and response were bleak, telling me that Douglas was somewhere near the Cambodian border, with a few other prisoners, all of them moved from camp to camp so that the location was never exactly known.

"Goodbye, then," he said, appearing strained, as though he were the one hurting; or could that just have been my wistful supposition? Finally, as simply as that, he turned and once more walked away. I stood, then leaned against the tree and watched him diminish as he moved away from me and then disappeared among people further up the avenue. When I could no longer see him, I felt real pain. Extreme anguish absolutely has a physical component, and pain seemed to be suffocating me. I could barely breathe and could not see clearly. Excruciated I was, not just within my heart that once loved but deep within my bones, right into the marrow. So, my legs collapsed and, having just been leaning against the tree, I slowly slid to the ground. An old woman passing by asked if I was all right. I told her that I was fine, only resting a minute or two. Another lie for a miserable day. But after a bit, ignoring stares from people passing on the sidewalk, I rose and, although staggering, managed to enter my car.

So, we had spoken, not as we should have long years before, but finally for the last time, and I had learned more than I expected or ever imagined. I always thought our love would be forever, but now I understood that forever is never as long or constant as we hope.

Frank was finally really gone, out of sight; gone for good or bad, but completely gone.

CHAPTER 11

Purple Horizon

F rom that street-side encounter onward, I threw myself, immersed myself, drowned myself, within work. I actually increased the number of venues for singing, my driver bringing me from one restaurant or club on to the next, three or four songs, no more than that and no encores. I would be so exhausted on returning home that my mother and friend Kim Chi would need to help me to bed. Mother feared that overexertion, the constant exhaustion, might affect my throat and throw me back in the hospital. Gradually, I slowed what had been a frenetic pace.

I received the award for best Viet Nam actress in early 1970, endorsed by the Movie Producers Association and presented by President Nguyen Van Thieu. I had many years previously met President Thieu and his wife in Rach Gia when he was a field commander, so the ceremony was friendly as well as respectful. Some observers were surprised that we had a rather extended conversation. A few of those attending remarked among themselves, to appear knowledgeable about my affairs, that I was already working in a new feature film, *Chan Troi Tim* (The Purple Horizon).

Chan Troi Tim was the first "mega" financial movie for Viet Nam and the first filmed entirely in CinemaScope and Eastmancolor. The

Receiving the award for best actress from President Thieu.

projected cost would have been prohibitive for any single producer or studio, so a cooperative consortium of investors supported the venture. The number of strong personalities involved meant there was considerable debate among them regarding cast selection. There were at least two other actresses considered for the lead role, and one even began accumulating an appropriate wardrobe. Ultimately, my

Sharing a moment with President Thieu at a reception following the award ceremony.

selection, director Hoang Hoa told me, was made by a group consensus on the basis of sex appeal and because my popular reputation
as a sultry nightclub singer seemed congruent with the film character. It was ironic, therefore, that within the film all "my" singing

With Nguyen thi Mai Anh, wife of President Thieu, at the reception.

The rather famous nude painting featured in my best-known film.

was done by Thai Thanh, whose clear voice was most suitable for the production recording equipment!

The script was adapted from a popular novel whose title referred to the horizon's frequently appearing a beautiful deep violet at the final moment of sunset. The story was a sensitive one for me, as the role I assumed was that of a nightclub singer entangled in the Saigon milieu who loved a soldier committed to his comrades in combat, so both were doomed to a barely tolerable separate existence. The secret parallel with my own dilemma was the painful basis for a heartfelt performance. During production I provided the first "semi-nude" scene in Vietnamese commercial film, as the script required posing for an actor/artist who was painting my portrait. The actual painter was a woman, Truong Thi Thinh, and her work nearly mirror images the famous late eighteenth-century "La Maja desnuda" by Goya. I have that painting, the film portrait, with me today; it hangs in a guest room. Many a visitor has asked the favor of being allowed to purchase it. I always respond, "Maybe someday, but I don't know when."

The situation for our Republic of Viet Nam through spring and summer 1970 did not seem so alarming as it had five years, or even two years, previously. I thought the national elections three years before had really laid a foundation for citizens'—that is, the general population's—participation in our own southern government. Yes, there were problems (for instance, President Thieu did overreach in some respects), but opposition newspapers, assembly representatives, and senators were allowed a voice, so all my Saigon friends believed that what we had in the south was absolutely preferable to one-party communist, even if nationalist communist, dictatorial rule. A negative crosscurrent seemed indicated by the arrest and imprisonment of general secretary of the National Assembly's lower house Tran Ngoc Chau,[12] but many people voiced an expectation

---

[12] Tran Ngoc Chau, born in Hue, was a Viet Minh combatant and later graduate of the Dalat Military Academy where he was a good friend to Nguyen Van Thieu. He was

that he should be, and so eventually would be, released. There was even an independent film, *Dat Kho* (The Sorrowful Land), featuring popular artist and songwriter Trinh Cong Son,[13] just beginning production with a general anti-war theme. Nothing remotely like that would ever have been allowed even a beginning under communist governance.

The environment, economic and social as much as political, seemed stable, but I was a little apprehensive due to an awareness that the continuing departure of American military units would expose vulnerabilities. Our military, above all else the land army, would have to defend everywhere and would be thus overextended by needing to compensate for the absence of allied battalions and regiments. I wondered whether our resources could support a sufficient increased number of men in uniform so that we could organize a strategic reaction force. And, I feared, the departure of the American army would allow some politicians in the imperial city on the Potomac to calculate my country less important than had originally been supposed. So, although there was surface calm, I foresaw potential, even probable, turbulence.

I had been drifting, but now my sixth sense caused me to reconsider our family options. There was at least some possibility of national instability. I needed to seek contingency "tickets out" for myself, my children, and my parents. Now, because of a chance street-side meeting, I was finally severed from the gray-green eyed echo of the past. I could scrutinize, carefully, the foreign suitors who clustered around in nightclubs and at receptions. It was as though they were auditioning before me as I had previously auditioned for advertising, singing engagements, and stage and film roles.

---

highly regarded by President Diem; he twice served as province chief in Ben Tre and once as Danang mayor. His memoir was published by Texas Tech University Press in 2012.

[13] Trinh Cong Son was a popular songwriter and performer who underscored the pain felt by everyone, but especially rural folk, trapped within war.

There was, it seemed, a limitless number of embassy officers and businessmen who enthusiastically professed love and desire to carry me away to live happily ever after. But almost all of them balked at shouldering my three children, and the mention of my parents seemed to freeze their previously ardent smiles.

One persistent admirer, Robert Henry, did commit to my bringing the children with me in a family package, and he promised to take Mother and Father from Viet Nam if circumstances someday required their joining us. Bob worked for one of the large American contractor companies; I think it may have been Pacific Architects and Engineers. That company, like all the others, profited by performing tasks that the US Army had done for itself in other wars. Bob Henry's company alone had hundreds of American employees in Viet Nam, as did other major corporations. Bob, like all the American contractors, was well paid and nicely housed in a fine home provided by the company. He was consistently persuasive, and I trusted his promise never to abandon my family members. As a test of his character, I moved into his residence. The situation was a departure from all that I had been used to, but tolerable. Obvious to any of those who knew me well, he was definitely not the man of my dreams; but at specific critical moments our lives require adjustment to reality.

We did have difficulties. Bob was a short man and could hardly match me in height when I wore high-heeled shoes for singing performances. I was extremely uncomfortable with him physically, in every way; moreover, we did not even slightly match emotionally. We had no common interests, really nothing to talk about. He was unreasonably jealous, manifested not only by his traveling from café to café each evening when I sang but also in focusing much more on my response to the audience than to the audience's response to me. He even insisted on following me to sessions with my singing coach when I needed to work on a new arrangement.

But while insecure and suspicious, he was also proud of having captured me, the unobtainable Kim Vui, who was thought most desirable by other men. In Saigon, that short man attained stature by association with me, appearing in every audience, somewhat possessively, when I sang. He even bragged of his conquest to friends, some of whom later in confidence repeated every word to me.

The reality of the American military reduction was more obvious late that same year. Although evidenced by less raucous Saigon streets, and surely reflected on some situation maps, our Republic of Viet Nam Armed Forces expanded and were finally better equipped by our American ally. The rate of the American departure from Viet Nam was not yet so precipitous as to erode the general population's confidence, our economy, or our expectations. And the American contractor presence in Saigon clubs and restaurants did not diminish. In fact, I had the impression that the number of those well-paid civilians might even have increased for a time. They strutted proudly, in absence of real combatants, and seemed even more boisterous than when originally assigned as "war contractors" supplementary to "war fighters."

Unfortunately, the general atmosphere was also one wherein all the players believed that "money rules." Saigon seemed ever more tainted by corruption, and I feared the stain would spread as "important people" frequently hosted parties for each other, competing to see which would be the most lavish. As an actress and singer, perhaps the most prominent entertainer of the day, I could not avoid frequent attendance. A popular song of the time refrained *"Saigon dep lam, Saigon oi, Saigon oi"* (Saigon so beautiful, oh Saigon, oh Saigon), but I thought it might really be otherwise, and many Vietnamese who had experienced the expanding gap between hamlets and city would have agreed with me.

Today, many of the Viet Nam diaspora, first or second generation, have adopted a spurious nostalgia, one might even suggest "delusion," for an imagined bright and scintillating "old Saigon" that was romantic, intriguing, and twinkling, especially by late night. Sometimes, naively, they even use the term "Catinat" to label a contemporary business enterprise, ignorant of the original French intention to insult.[14] From the Arc en Ciel dance hall and restaurant in Cho Lon, past the Bong Lai rooftop restaurant on Le Loi Avenue, to bars along Tu Do Street, the girls who played hostess were circumstantially available, some trafficked, and some addicted. Most of them had fled difficult rural situations created or exacerbated by war. We should all ponder the cautionary reminder that "all that glitters is not gold."

Public nightlife was not a venue for political dealing and intrigue, even though such players circulated among clubs and theaters. Plans and schemes were advocated, altered, approved, or discarded inside special premises like the Viet Nam Air Force Club at Tan Son Nhut or within the secure walls of the presidential office. Manipulators and schemers might subsequently celebrate in public but would first sketch and hatch plots elsewhere. There was no *Casablanca*-reminiscent "Rick's Café" in Saigon.

Early in 1971, President Thieu approved a great, by aspiration as much as size, multi-battalion cross-border operation into southern Laos by our military forces. Airborne, Marine, First Division, and Ranger units were all involved. Our newspapers and radio/television outlets (government-supported, therefore government amplifiers) all reported initial progress and success. Even Tchepone, crossroad of the communist party's logistical system from North Viet Nam through Laos, was at least temporarily occupied by our army. Gradually we found out that the operation was launched at American insistence and was entirely dependent on American helicopter insertions and air support. Then much more slowly we found out that the entire effort on the ground was poorly coordinated and poorly commanded; the resulting loss of good soldiers, junior officers, and major equipment was astounding.

---

[14] When nineteenth-century French naval forces shelled Danang, and later Gia Dinh, to secure control of Viet Nam, the one vessel that participated at both locations was the warship *Catinat*. Later, the French secret police headquarters for Saigon were located on upper Catinat Street not far from the more recognizable Saigon Cathedral.

How did we learn the extent of the bad news, the distressing reality? Well, almost every disaster will have survivors, and they cannot be silenced for long. Survivors have no reason to exaggerate; a simple description suffices to stun listeners. The fortunate ones who escaped made their way, some by helicopter and some by foot, rearward to safety. They spoke with friends who repeated horrific stories to others. Wounded soldiers conversed with family and staff in hospitals. Some families were notified that their fathers, husbands, or sons were among the missing so that, more quickly than you might think, the painful truth, just as it had in 1965, filtered south to the capital.

My feelings were mixed. Why would the Americans have planned, pushed, and logistically supported a venture into Laos that they themselves were previously unwilling to attempt? Could our president have been so uninformed that he believed the senior regional commander could manage that kind of responsibility? The end result of this calamity could not be anything but encouraging for our enemy, the communist party, both in the Paris negotiations and perhaps subsequently on the battlefield.

Despite that long February and March disaster, what passed for normal civilian life—that is, by Saigon standards—continued unabated. *Chanh Troi Tim* was a sensation when released in 1971 by the Lien Anh Motion Picture Company. There was an immediate impact on Saigon streets. Where a poster was attached to pole or tree for advertising a specific theater showing, people would gather, and someone might slyly take that poster down and away as a souvenir. Tickets were sold out as soon as cinema houses opened their cashiers' windows. There were mini riots when people who had struggled in line were informed that showings were sold out, so they could only return another day to stand in line again. My picture was on the cover of every popular magazine, and I dared not accompany my mother to market. Twice we were almost crushed by autograph seekers and other Saigon folk who seemed intent on touching my arms, my face, even grabbing at my clothing.

The host of a popular Saigon television show, *Nguoi Dan Muon Biet* (The People Want to Know) asked me, during an interview program with actresses Kieu Chinh and Tham Thuy Hang, whether I thought the nude portrait scene was in any way unclean. I replied by asking whether he, while viewing the film, had thought it beautiful or dirty. After responding that he personally thought the scene beautiful, I suggested that in life, beauty or ugliness depends on the observer and reveals the conditioned mind of that person.

Importantly, especially thinking back fifty years, the film did portray more than my sex appeal. It provided Saigon audiences some visualization of the sacrifice, for their benefit, made by combat soldiers in the field. Perceptive viewers would also notice the malfeasance of a rear area staff officer who improperly, and to benefit himself, issued field assignments to other soldiers; there is one odd, fleeting reference to the 1963 coup that assassinated a president. While my role was conceived as essentially a romantic one, it also illustrated the precarious position of women who might be importuned into a regrettable relationship, and many Vietnamese women could relate to that situation. *Chan Troi Tim* was awarded the prize for Best Artistic Expression in June 1971 at the Asian Film Festival in Taipei.

And even now, when I've matured to the status of "senior citizen," the enduring popularity of that story and my cinematic role continues to amaze me. In 2018, *Chan Troi Tim* was screened at a film festival in California. I think two or three hundred people attended, and dozens lingered to converse with me before going home.

Unlike other films within which I played a part, I do have a copy of *Chanh Troi Tim* in 90-minute DVD format, and I appreciate the My Van Film Company having provided me with that gift. Whatever was really happening within our unending war, many Vietnamese and Americans were making contingent arrangements. Wealthy, or well-connected, Vietnamese, even senior military officers, bribed or called up favors to facilitate their own children's departure for foreign study. Americans, especially contractor profiteers, sensitive to the potential shrinkage of opportunity, discussed employment opportunities in other countries.

Bob Henry did not want to delay marriage and confuse an eventual departure with a need to make simultaneous complicated family arrangements. I still hesitated, experiencing uncomfortable feelings, regrets . . . realizing from sharing the same house that his being about three years younger than I was not insignificant. Maturity is not age-dependent, but in his case that did appear to somewhat apply. However, pausing on the diving tower of life is a futile postponement of what must, and will, be done. I could not further delay my decision and had no alternative for my family. So, we held our wedding ceremony on August 17, 1971. More than 300 guests attended a reception where Bob fairly strutted as if a proud monarch. And here is a surprise for you: that date was also Frank's birthday. Simple coincidence, or deliberate exorcism?

The next month, President Thieu was reelected, but this time he was unopposed by any other candidate. His new vice-presidential partner was Tran Van Huong, a respectable older southern-origin political figure. That was encouraging for some of us, but although I did vote for President Thieu, the lack of competition was confusing. Was it because no one else felt qualified? Was it because other political figures doubted the integrity of the process? Did many simply believe that it made no difference who would be president? Politically interested friends debated but could not reach any consensus.

After the election, and I think simply coincidental, the economy seemed to subside more precipitously. The steady withdrawal of American military was, in economic terms, draining money from our markets and family incomes. Readers should not be surprised. Large American military bases employed many Vietnamese, and around those bases free markets thrived. Young American Marines and soldiers spent their own money—lots, by our standards—not often wisely, but liberally. Now there were also fewer Vietnamese employed by American military units and contractors, so there was a consequent precipitous decline of dollars propping up a frail piaster economy.

I do not recall a late 1971 sense, or even intimation, of panic; but this child of strife was apprehensive of a sea change beneath the surface calm. An ephemeral purple horizon at sunset seemed probable for the Republic of Viet Nam.

CHAPTER 12

Farewell, Viet Nam

T he Communist Party of Viet Nam, national party of a three-region country but headquartered in the north and with a small, disciplined core directed by a central-region leadership, ordered a massive conventional attack against the southern region–based Republic of Viet Nam early in 1972. Admittedly, from the first republic organized by Ngo Dinh Diem through military-led administrations, leading to and including the second republic established by elected president Nguyen Van Thieu, there had always been sporadic internal resistance against the Republic of Viet Nam, whether ignited by former Viet Minh or by tribal or religious dissidents. But from 1958 and 1959 onward, rebellion to eliminate the southern government was organized and directed by the Hanoi-based national communist party.

Through 1963, maybe even into early 1964, most of the communist combatants were of southern origin—that is, south of the Ben Hai River demilitarized zone. Even so, the political cadre and supply and supplementary specialists were sent from the north, and there was never any doubt as to Hanoi being the point of command and control. The national communist party used the northern region population to form a draftee-based army to support southern operations and to prepare for a contingent invasion of the south. My understanding, from conversation with Vietnamese and American friends, is that from 1965 onward, matching the arrival of regular American (and other countries') military formations, Hanoi sent northern draftee-formed regiments and divisions southward to supplement the military units of the self-named *Mat tran Dan toc Giai phong mien Nam Viet Nam* (National Liberation Front of South Viet Nam).

During the 1968 Tet Offensive, the more local, native to the south, ostensible "liberation" units and political cadre were ordered to the forefront of attack into urban areas—not just Saigon, but almost every province capital, too. They were ground down by Republic of Viet Nam and American counterattack and related follow-on combat, forcing a communist withdrawal to base areas. Consequently, from 1970 onward the main forces' burden of combat on behalf of the communist party was necessarily, almost entirely, taken up by northern soldiers drafted by the Hanoi government, trained, organized, and dispatched southward.

The spring 1972 attack was widespread but most intensely concentrated at four points. First, there was an open flagrant strike through the demarcation area between North and South, into Quang Tri Province, with subsequent loss of that province capital. Second was a major attack originating from bases in Laos, over the border, and into Kontum Province. Third, existing communist forces in northern Binh Dinh and southern Quang Ngai of central coastal Viet Nam overran some government positions and interdicted two major highways, Routes 1 and 19. The fourth major attack, from bases in the Cambodian border region, seized Loc Ninh town and encircled the province capital An Loc.

Through the next several weeks our Republic of Viet Nam soldiers, after the initial shock, distinguished themselves by holding, counterattacking, and recovering almost all lost ground. But there were problems. Although Quang Tri was recovered, highways in

Central Viet Nam were cleared, and Kontum was held, the encirclement at An Loc was not broken, and it was obvious that American air power was absolutely necessary for the future survival of our independent republic.

I ask readers to pardon that brief sketch of military action if it holds no interest for you, but I believe that your comprehension of those events is necessary to understanding the road that I continued to follow, for the benefit of my family. My own situational awareness was the basis for all the decisions that I subsequently made. You may think my analysis surprisingly sophisticated, but it was not difficult to deduce, even from slanted official media statements, the true conditions that prevailed. Friends in our military, staff officers, and, even more significantly, some of those returning temporarily from points of combat shared their opinions with me. And remember, I was exposed while a young girl to countryside realities. No gauze veil shielded my eyes.

That spring my one sure conviction was that the future not only appeared difficult but was undeniably bleak and not likely to improve. A previous sense of an achieved stalemate now seemed to be illusion, as I sensed that the fundamental resolve of the communist party for unification of north and south was undiluted. Our own southern region's resolve to attain a balance of forces as a platform for coexistence would be short-lived and would likely evaporate if the American government's conducting of secret negotiations with Vietnamese communists in Paris became entirely self-interested at our expense.

The United States had already withdrawn almost all the combat forces that had saved Viet Nam in 1965 and 1968. Once the very few remaining were taken home, it would be unlikely that America would continue constant air warfare not in direct support of young American soldiers on the ground. America, in the end, would do what would be thought best for America, honor be damned, and I knew in my heart that the American decision would probably not be good for my country, the Republic of Viet Nam.

I was not mistrusting Americans because of the one who had separated from me. In fact, I learned from Kim Chi, who once saw him in downtown Saigon with his Taiwanese wife and son, that he was back in Viet Nam. I would have bet all my quail egg money that he was as seldom in safe Saigon city as he had been years past. Douglas Ramsey, the personable young man who had introduced us nine years before, was still a prisoner, six years already, somewhere in the Cambodian border jungle. Another of Frank's friends had been killed in Laos three years previously. Now we learned from Vietnamese newspapers that his sort of "uncle," John Vann, had met his own, perhaps inevitable, end near Kontum a few weeks past.

My respect for those Americans I knew, and all others whom I had not met but who in one way or another responded to a call for service at risk to their lives and who had done their best in shattering situations, was unsurpassed. But I also definitely understood, from my brief travel in America and speaking with Americans in Saigon, that Washington leaders, President Nixon and his male muse Henry Kissinger, now thought we Vietnamese and our country too complex, too mystifying, "a tough nut that can't be cracked," and therefore constituting an unacceptably costly project.

America, I was sure, would withdraw from Viet Nam. My film roles with subtle anti-communist themes would make me a pariah if the Communist Party achieved unification and established a dictatorship by bitter central committee. My family, especially the children, would suffer because of some amorphous "people's judgement" passed against me. Even though it was necessary to depart my country, and convinced as I was that the United States would abandon Viet Nam, I should not and would not abandon my family. Just as my mother had saved Father and me in 1945, now almost thirty years later it was my turn, my responsibility, to save the family. So, whatever my own mixed personal feelings, the choice to marry Bob Henry did provide an immediate lifeline for my children, and eventually for Mother and Father.

And I was pregnant! Initially that pregnancy became an issue between Bob and me, because a jealous person who envied my cinematic success and the ease with which I established a lifeline for myself and my three children whispered incessantly to Bob that I had a secret lover whom I frequently met when away from the house to work on arrangements with my singing coach. We had an awkward few weeks before Bob realized that the poisonous lie did not accord with his daily observation of reality.

Bob was offered, and he was considering, a position in Guam where his company had a major contract to support American military facilities. I did not know where Guam was located, but after checking a world map was comforted by seeing the island was a partial step, although not halfway, in the direction to continental America. Unaware of what other opportunities might later be available for Bob, unsure whether my opinion would even have any weight, I encouraged my young husband to commit to the move.

Speaking honestly, so long as I was with my children in Viet Nam, I did not feel that the marriage of convenience/necessity with Bob was insoluble. I could restore my independence without much difficulty. But once uprooted from Viet Nam, my life circumstances would be very much at the mercy of another.

I should not inadvertently convey any impression that this choice was easy or formed by an entirely rational decision-making process. I was as temped to indulge in wishful thinking as were any of my fellow citizens. My public popularity in 1971 and 1972 was at a high point, unmatched by that of any other performer. Magazines with my photographs sold out. Newspapers reported every imaginable detail of my life, some cleverly discovered by diligent reporters and others entirely fictive penned by inventive scribblers. I am still grateful that a widely read journalist, Trong Minh, in extensively circulated Saigon magazines and newspapers, always published corrective articles protecting my reputation. Regardless of the accuracy or inaccuracy of what was written, there was a reading audience for every story. It was impossible for me to enter any market unobserved. Crowds would quickly form, fans would call for autographs, and people would press so close that produce displays sometimes tumbled down.

On one occasion the reaction, the intensity, of people around my car was so great that my driver could not protect an open door for me, and only by police intervention were we able to depart. Even then, the pressure on the car door before I had gotten completely inside so pinched my leg that I had to seek treatment for injury. I was still frequently singing, to maintain a steady income, and sometimes would be pursued from venue to venue by journalists or admirers in their own cars. My driver could usually outwit those enthusiasts by altering our route, but on a few occasions Kim Chi or another companion girlfriend needed to interpose as a screen while I would exit the car to enter the next nightclub on our schedule.

Organizing for departure from Viet Nam was easy for an American employed by one of the largest military contractors in the world. Bob's procedure was simple because Viet Nam entry and exit visa requirements were managed by an officer in the US Consulate responsible for assisting contractors. My situation, as a citizen of Viet Nam, even with a passport, was difficult. The first step, after approval for a United States visa arranged by the US Consulate, would be travel to Guam for expeditious nationalization, swearing allegiance to America as a new citizen.

But having a Viet Nam passport with an entry visa for the US was just the beginning. I was also required to obtain a Republic of Viet Nam exit visa allowing departure from my country of birth. One would think that step a simple matter, but very little is easily accomplished in a country wherein law and regulation is at the whim of administrators. Obtaining the exit visa for myself, and subsequently for my children, amounted to hurdling potentially painful obstacles. My personal circumstances were more perilous than those for most other applicants. Although the Ministry of Foreign

Affairs would issue the departure visa, the office in question was headed by a lecherous army officer on detail to the ministry. He sent a message informing me that he held my file with approval pending and could provide the exit visa at my convenience, by meeting him in Vung Tau at the resort hotel owned by his good friends General and Madam Cao Van Vien.[15]

A rather common form of senior officer corruption at the time was to acquire ownership of hotel properties for lease to Americans, always expeditiously arranged by the wives so as to preserve the fiction of general officer probity. Setting the meeting place at Cao Van Vien's hotel in Vung Tau communicated in subtext that the lecher was well connected and expected that my gratitude should be expressed by granting romantic play. However, I was accompanied by an escort, my youngest son Khai, gangly and cranky from the hot two-hour drive from Saigon. The importuning rascal holding my file and exit visa met us in the reception area and, irritated that I was holding onto my son, insisted that my little boy could be cared for by the hotel reception staff while I accompanied him to a private room to discuss my case. Khai was tired, appeared feverish, and, since I surreptitiously pinched him occasionally so that he wailed a bit, he obviously could not be entrusted to others. Frustrated, the dirty officer threw the file with the exit visa on the floor and told me to go. I was happy to do that, and with my young escorting son in tow abandoned the sexual predator to some solitary hotel pleasure.

Hurdle leaped, in April I traveled to Guam, alone, to become an American citizen. I was about three months pregnant, but the air travel was not arduous and I arrived safely. There was a bit of a problem due to the hotel being overbooked and therefore my placement was to an exterior unit in a row of bungalows to the rear of the

---

[15] General Cao Van Vien, reputedly fearless when commanding airborne forces, eventually rose to the position of Chief of the Joint General Staff responsible for implementing President Thieu's directives. Profitable side ventures were masked by his avaricious spouse.

hotel proper. Two men seemed to observe me closely and then drift along behind me toward my lodging. Apprehensive, I notified the lobby desk, communicated my concern, and asked that my security be a priority. I did not see those men again. What I interpreted as uncomfortable attention may have been coincidental, but a woman traveling alone in strange surroundings cannot be too careful.

Planning is the foundation for success. A few weeks earlier in Saigon I had paid a bilingual Vietnamese army officer to coach me through preparation for the naturalization examination. I missed only one question and returned to Saigon in May 1972 as a new American.

Several friends, among them Vietnamese and some American colleagues of Bob, continued to invite us to dinners and receptions. But that echo of the past was already receding as I began to focus my attention and energy on the procedure for bringing my three children, born in Viet Nam, home to America.

Making travel arrangements for daughter Le Thu, plus sons Bao and Khai, was challenging. Bao was now 13 years old, and I was warned that in accordance with the spirit of mobilization laws he might not be allowed to depart the country. Like other rules and government decrees, enforcement was lax, at least with respect to rich families and sons of generals. But we could not take chances. The future for my country appeared dim and grim, so each birthday for Bao was a further incentive for departure.

Completing passport, exit visa, and American visa requirements for the two boys was a smooth process. Compiling documentation for Le Thu was more complicated because of her post-birth health problems and subsequent multiple hospitalizations while still a little girl. Obtaining the health examination/report required for American immigrant visa approval was difficult. She had been under the care of numerous physicians and clinics. You may not need this reminder, but I must note that this was before health-care providers maintained electronic files, which on the best of days can move records instantly from point to point and print with ease. Everything needed those many years ago had to be obtained in "hard copy" and could only be accomplished by multiple office visits with taxi travel back and forth.

And I was not even in Saigon! Just at that critical time, Bob needed to report for his new job in Guam, and he wanted to be sure that my pregnancy was carried to term for delivering birth on American soil. So, with my emotional distress rising, we left Le Thu and the boys temporarily with my father and mother in early September while transferring to Guam.

Our first child together, my fourth, was born in a Guam hospital. We named her Catherine. Bob had been previously troubled, even accusing, because of the spiteful whispers of another woman in Saigon. But when Cathy emerged, she was in facial appearance a tiny duplicate of Bob! The emotional impact of all that I was experiencing, and some possible postpartum depression, put me in a tailspin. I felt misjudged and mistreated, and I deeply missed and was agonizingly concerned for Le Thu, Bao, and Khai, left behind in Viet Nam. My constant worry was only relieved by the notification that all requirements for my three Viet Nam children were satisfied, and they could soon travel together to join me in Guam. I was fortunate to have had the assistance of Miss Hoa, whom we called "Hoa Y Ta," an attractive young nurse who was a friend of many years. She was the key, an absolutely indispensable and indefatigable person, who helped me during that desperate time of need, accumulating all the required medical documentation for Bao, Khai, and, especially, Le Thu.

Disconnection from their land of birth was not unduly upsetting for them. Children, at least during the pre-teen years, are infinitely flexible so long as they believe a competent adult is leading. However, separation from our birthplace was more difficult for me. Memories of my own childhood, civic action missions in hamlets, singing and cinema, a lost love, all surfaced each night and allowed only restless, semiconscious sleep. Staying the chosen course would have been unbearable had I not completely committed to what would be best for Le Thu, Bao, and Khai. While previously deeply rooted, especially by the children, and still resident in Viet Nam, my marriage to Bob Henry was not irreversible. Now, by following through on my own plan for a multistage movement of my family to America, I was in effect marriage-indentured by having obtained better prospects for children and a promise of refuge for Mother and Father if necessary.

Employment circumstances for my husband in Guam, while he was working as engineer for a contracting firm, were momentarily stable. The potential hitch, as I think far back, was that much of the company work, and the island economy in general, was predicated on the lavishness of defense spending. After the departure of combat units from Viet Nam, but with continuing American involvement, Guam was still a critical forward operating base, particularly for B-52 missions. And those B-52s did fly and fly, especially that 1972 December.

Soon after Cathy's birth I heard Americans on Guam speaking among themselves about President Nixon and his foreign policy advisor, Mr. Kissinger. They were said to have already made an agreement with the Viet Nam Communist Party for complete American military withdrawal from the south of Viet Nam.

I listened carefully to those late 1972 conversations and so learned that Hanoi, the command point for the Communist Party, would be allowed to keep military units in the south, within the Republic of Viet Nam . . . and even resupply and replace personnel! Was that really what we, anti-communist Vietnamese and Americans, had fought so many years to secure, acquiescence to the legitimacy of Hanoi military establishment in the South? My distaste, akin to acid reflux, for what seemed Nixon and Kissinger's politically convenient betrayal of sacrificed Americans and Vietnamese was not soothed by learning that President Thieu, insulted by the lack of American diplomatic finesse, had at first refused to sign. The document ostensibly negotiated on the behalf of the Republic of Viet Nam was only available (an indicator of Kissinger's attitude, or incompetence) in English.

Equally piqued by Kissinger's inept Saigon follow-through, Hanoi in retaliation suggested some cosmetic alterations. Awkward back-and-forth verbal jabbing failed to break the impasse, so the B-52s flew again and again until, with President Thieu somewhat mollified, an agreement for American military withdrawal was signed with Hanoi, wholly lacking any significant concessions on the part of the Viet Nam Communist Party.

My only slight consolation was derived from reading a newspaper account that described a recovery team taking almost two dozen American prisoners from a communist detention camp at Loc Ninh near the Cambodian border. The story included a list of the fortunate, and Douglas Ramsey was one of them. I was sure, not unreasonably, that Frank was involved. For just that moment—well, perhaps more than a moment—I rejoiced for the two of them, and even felt myself a small part of a special circle again. I always had a particularly fond memory of Douglas, and not only because he was the connector between me and Frank. He was an extraordinary American who could speak Vietnamese as we of that country did among ourselves.

America still has a significant defense role in Asia, and the B-52 may still be the big neighborhood policeman. While those B-52s roost in Guam, the military command, with associated contractors, will always be an important cog and gear in the Guam economy. I observed that there is a hospitable homegrown Guam society based on the indigenous Chamorro people. But more than forty years ago, the "contractor culture" and economy, derivative of the island-based B-52 representing far-away continental political America, dominated all. The uniformed American presence in Guam was a guarantor of the political relationship between island governance and

Washington. When receptions were organized for any ceremonial event, the presence of senior Air Force officers was as important as attendance by the governor and mayor.

Contracting companies competed to host the best parties. This was at least partly to curry favor with contract-issuing government officers who would also report the progress and execution of each contract. Bob and I were always in demand as guests because, once recovered from Cathy's delivery, and after settling my other children in a school routine, I accepted a contract in early 1973 to sing at a major Agana hotel nightclub. The band was from the Philippines, and they were conversant with all the American classics of that era. Some consequent popularity, maybe even notoriety, meant that our attendance at social events provided a sort of special flavor. Bob was pleased because my image was beneficial to himself. He basked in my reflection.

He could have "left well enough alone" but was unable to refrain from trying to assume a managerial role. He collected my salary and held it himself, because, he explained, he was responsible for the family finances. I did not resist that presumption because, after all, he really had kept his promise to bring all my children to America. But he failed to understand that what might seem to be low take-home renumeration was due to his frequently charging drinks for his attending friends. His behavior finally brought my resumption of singing to an end. When the original nightclub contract concluded, Bob, self-designated manager, insisted on handling the renewal. What should have been a simple extension was snarled by Bob taking an "either increase the salary or we walk" approach that aggravated the club owner, management, and me. The owner told Bob, basically, to take a walk. The overall unpleasantness was distressing for me personally.

As consequence of Bob having completely fudged the contract renewal, a heavy depression, like a thick blanket, enveloped me. I was deprived of the opportunity for artistic expression and was consequently resentful of my husband's intervention. My modest income had helped with household expenses; now family finances were constricted. With no household help I was responsible for cleaning, meals, and care for the children. My three recently arrived from Viet Nam were entering school. It was not easy for them: new classes and teachers, new classmates, and, above all, new language. Cathy, still an infant, required much attention. My burden, I felt, was great. Dark shadows, it seemed, gathered around and pressed upon me.

All the news from Viet Nam, and letters from friends, were discouraging. I was apprehensive for my mother's safety while simultaneously recognizing that my own emotional state was fragile. Bringing my mother to Guam right away, rather than eventually, was a desirable immediate solution for both problems. Bob, as I have always acknowledged and appreciated, despite our problematic marital circumstances moved swiftly to make arrangements for Mother to join us in Guam. There was one comic aspect to her departure from Viet Nam. She was able to convert some savings to jewelry, time-honored international practice for refugees; but at the time of her departure from Saigon she still had, even given the market exchange rate, bundles of piasters. So, she arrived in Agana in early September 1973 toting a small suitcase stuffed with Vietnamese money that was worthless . . . other than serving as an entertaining family story.

Having my mother with me again did make a positive difference for everyone in our home. Her assistance with cleaning and cooking allowed me more time to mother newly born Cathy. Meanwhile, Le Thu, Bao and Khai, my three from Viet Nam, made rapid progress in school. We processed adoption and name changes for them to facilitate adaption to a new national environment and culture. Le Thu became Anne, Bao took the name David, and Khai was now Anthony, all with the Henry family name.

Almost immediately, indirectly derived from the previous singing engagement, a new financial opportunity unexpectedly but happily emerged to engage my creative instinct and time. The wives and girlfriends of prominent residents, who had frequently attended performances in the nightclub or met Bob and me at receptions, had often asked where I obtained my evening gowns. I would proudly reply that my dresses were designed by myself, tailored in Saigon, and later refreshed by alterations in Guam. They would typically express amazement at my ability, especially given the time required, to creatively gown myself for performances. Now many of those ladies discovered that I was no longer singing every evening, and a few asked whether it would be possible for me to create special clothing for them. I responded positively, not simply to be polite but more particularly to seize a new opportunity for independent income. My mother enthusiastically encouraged me and helped with shears and long stints at the sewing machine. We worked with material available locally in Adana, mostly fabrics and threads imported from Hong Kong and the Philippines.

We wasted nothing. From bolts of material—silks, cottons, and other fabrics—we brought forth clothing that would not have shamed angels. There would always be leftover material, "odds and ends," from which we would challenge ourselves to fashion something complimentary and useful: scarves, gloves, or occasionally small evening purses.

We thought demand would be consistently high. I had not realized that after several months of socially prominent women competing to see who would wear a new creation before anyone else, there would be a subsequent reduction of demand due to a finite customer base. We were able to "work down" our stock of material for dresses, blouses, and slacks at no loss of investment, and then I needed to seek a new opportunity for family income.

A friend suggested opening a small gift shop that would attract tourists frequenting downtown Agana. There was a sort of souvenir business with an existing property lease that was immediately available, and I could take it over for what seemed a reasonable sum. The owner was from India and had titled the store SAMBO, explaining to me that it was a form of martial art, originating in Russia but very popular in Guam. This sounded strange to me, but for simplicity of transfer I retained the business/shop name. Our customers included American military persons as well as the anticipated international travelers, many from Japan. We were doing well until street closure for construction to increase lanes as part of an Agana capital city improvement program impeded easy access. The work had long been scheduled but was not divulged to me by the previous business owner, and it had not occurred to me that more comprehensive inquiry would have been advisable. I was fortunate to sell the business at no loss to someone else who had both the patience and the wherewithal to wait out the road project completion.

There were still problems for me at home, and especially a major one within our family. My first, and always loved, daughter, Le Thu, was a teenager, and the Guam environment was nothing like the one that had enfolded me more than twenty years earlier. Even when she had been a very young girl in Viet Nam, she attracted male attention as honey draws flies. And, like many of her age, she was definitely curious about the male of our species. My mother and I had to be on guard constantly, and we even enlisted the help of her two young brothers to keep watch and report back to us. Despite our best effort, Le Thu slipped the bonds of family restraints and too soon ran away with a young American Marine, who like many men would pluck a flower wherever and whenever possible. She was gone, packing with never a word then out the door, and eventually moving to mainland America with her husband. I was miserable and worried for her.

Almost negligible by comparison were financial, and marital, problems with Bob. He spoke with me one day, surprisingly, about a loan needing repayment to a man from the Philippines. I knew nothing about a loan but supposed it could have been in connection with some property he purchased in the Agana hills, property that he had told me was in both our names. Mother was persuaded to yield two diamond rings, part of her refugee collection derived from my past Saigon income, as equivalent to the amount of money needed to repay funds that Bob had borrowed. So, it may have been in gratitude for this act, as much as in fulfillment of his promise, that in order to relieve my mother's sense of isolation and loneliness Bob succeeded in making arrangements for my father to leave Viet Nam and join us in February 1974. I made sure that Father would respond positively by discontinuing my occasional money remittance that had permitted his womanizing and gambling in Saigon.

Despite the depression stemming from Le Thu's absence, I obtained employment with a Japanese jewelry company, Haku-botan, and was just digging into that new endeavor when Saigon, the Saigon that I knew, fell to the Viet Nam Communist Party by the 1975 massive offensive commanded from Hanoi. Even as Viet-namese started escaping, American bases in Guam began preparations for receiving thousands of desperate people seeking refuge. Guam was about 2,500 miles distant from Saigon, approximately the distance from New York to Los Angeles, so simply on that point alone, receiving evacuees represented a tremendous challenge. There was no immediate alternative. Other countries were extremely reluctant to accept, even on a transit basis, large numbers of Vietnamese because ultimate forward destinations were not yet fixed.

The immediate number of Vietnamese fleeing, as best they could and by any means, to an indeterminate future elsewhere was far over 130,000 scrambling souls. More would have chosen to depart had there been sufficient warning and organization. Guam's governor Ricardo Bordallo very early, even while numbers were unclear, offered Guam as a relief and transit point. With many permanent base facilities, and an American talent for improvising, what would have been a logistical miracle anywhere else in the world was efficiently accomplished even as aircraft were landing and ships approaching.

Radio Station KUAM asked me to join their staff for broadcasting reassurance to approaching vessels and to provide a regular Vietnamese-language newscast each day for the hundreds, and soon thousands, who would be long-term sheltered, fed, and processed persons for onward movement to continental points where permanent relocation within America could be arranged. The Hakubotan Company kindly made me available to participate in that vast humanitarian undertaking. United States Army, Air Force, Navy, and Marine Corps personnel were energized to prepare Guam facilities to treat and temporarily house incoming waves of desperate Vietnamese. I visited those locations every day even while spending hours at the radio station.

I recall that the most quickly contrived reception and processing site was at the Camp Orote "tent city," set on what might have been an abandoned airfield, where old runways and taxiways were now avenues and streets for refugees. Walking through Orote, winding around tents, I often encountered people who had known me in Saigon long before. If there was an immediate need for a small amount of money, I provided it right away. People enthusiastically set up platforms upon which I could sit and speak by handheld megaphone to explain administrative notices. I encouraged everyone to look to the future, have courage, and retain a faith that, having come so far, they could surely build new lives in a new land. Strangely, speaking this way was also a form of self-therapy, as I knew that the advice so easily offered to others really needed to be applied to myself.

There were a few moments of levity. My good friend, journalist Trong Minh, as my mother had done earlier also carried with him life savings in a small satchel, entirely in Vietnamese currency and now entirely worthless. He laughed, himself, for having naively thought there might be currency conversion! I also met Vietnamese fishermen who had boarded an American naval vessel back home, thinking their own small boat would be quickly inspected then released, as in the past, so that they could continue fishing. Instead, amazed, they saw their own boat cut loose and abandoned, bobbing in the wake of the larger American ship, diminishing as the separation widened, then disappearing in the distance. They were on their way to America!

These, and others who had second or third thoughts, who had been caught up in moments of circumstantial panic, were eventually sorted for return to Viet Nam on a Vietnamese commercial ship, the *Thuong Tin*, that had been pressed into use for escape from Saigon. I shed tears for them, sure that they would not be compassionately treated on their return to Viet Nam, because no matter the excuse, they had in the first instance left rather than immediately welcomed unification. The communist party would not appreciate any explanation.

Those initial thousands of fortunate refugees were later moved forward to processing camps in Arkansas, California, Florida, and Pennsylvania. But Guam was the "first responder" and played an important role in convincing America at large that Vietnamese who had been abandoned deserved refuge and eventual embrace within America, this amazing country of complex national origins. Simultaneously, the Vietnamese refugees were convinced by Guam's example that in America they would be provided with considerate opportunity. All Vietnamese Americans, who within the quick passage of two or three generations will not feel hyphenated, should never forget that it was President Gerald Ford who pretty firmly determined that as many Vietnamese who wished and could make American shores one way or another should be accepted for resettlement. Regrettably, I believe, not all American political leaders would have made the same generous and righteous decision.

My impression was that about half the initial refugees were Catholic, reflective of a relatively privileged position the church had attained in the southern half of the country, and perhaps also a well-developed sense of cohesion and fear of the advancing communists. In succeeding years, about a million more people arrived either as "boat people" escaping a repressive regime or through an "orderly departure" system arranged between newly unified Viet Nam and the United States of America. Today, as I write, there are more than two million Americans of Vietnamese origin, quite a contrast with 1962 when there was only one Vietnamese restaurant in our entire fifty states!

For me personally, having found but later lost the only man truly loved, and now with my country of birth lost as well, I would learn that one can survive even in the absence of happiness.

CHAPTER 13

Escape from Tehran

W hat on this good earth was I doing in Tehran? Well, as previously noted, contractor employment in Guam for my husband Bob Henry was from the start linked to the American war effort in Viet Nam. But now in the middle of 1975, the B-52 was somewhat less a symbol of power and perhaps more indicative of frustration within a failed policy. Even so, and although the war was over, it was not feasible to draw down the island's military facilities without detailed planning. Thus, we had not moved from Guam right away. But it was clear we would not be staying on the island for long.

Bob was eventually able to connect himself to a position working for the Pentagon, perhaps based on his Army Reserve Officer status. Following our arrival in Virginia we purchased a house in Fairfax. Bob, of course, handled every part of the process. Although he was a little short of the amount necessary for the down payment, my mother and I were able to contribute that modest amount. Bob would don his uniform every day and proceed to an office building nearby that strangely shaped maze of military corridors on the Potomac. It seemed curious to see him, who had never fought a day in Viet Nam, dressed as though a real soldier. It looked very make-believe to me.

But Bob had brought my children with me as part of the marriage package, had moved my mother and father from Saigon to join us, and we had a daughter together in Guam. Despite some tension between the two of us, his having done all that he had promised was no small matter. Despite what happened later, I will always acknowledge and be grateful for his having kept that promise to me.

A second daughter with Bob, christened Jaime, was born in 1977 in Virginia. As with Cathy, our first in Guam, Bob was initially accusatory because at birth she appeared darker complexioned than he had expected. The doctors attempted to explain that there had been an umbilical cord problem having a temporary effect on her complexion, but my chronically insecure husband was cranky for a couple of days until time proved his reaction irrational. Those two days were hard psychologically because my mother was completely occupied with caring for the other four children and Bob was just short of hostile; my immediate emotional support was provided by the doctors and nursing staff who comforted me. I felt alone, solitary, even though Mother and Father were with me in Virginia.

Less than a year later, in May 1978, another daughter, Victoria, proved my fertility constant even while feeling miserable! Life on Guam had never seemed too distant from Viet Nam. But now on the east coast of the United States, I had to acknowledge, and to accept, a new reality. My country of birth, as I had known it, was lost to me forever.

I thought it advisable, in fact necessary, to learn a useful skill, so I enrolled in a dental technology class. It was extremely difficult because of course the instructional material was all in English, and I was not competent at the required professional level of comprehension. My "hands-on" skill, however, was at least equivalent to that of more advanced classmates and others would frequently ask me to help when working with model denture material. I even prepared a set of dentures for my mother, and she used them comfortably for the remainder of her life. Ultimately, although I liked the sub-ject, my insufficient language skill proved too heavy a handicap for obtaining certification.

Frustrated academically, and to secure some emotional consola-tion as well as a modest income, I did some occasional singing. Bob always accompanied me, a sort of looming presence. His famil-iar simmering jealousy whenever someone complimented a song soured every performance. I often felt unwell in head and stomach, something like the nausea experienced after an ill-advised day on amusement park rides. Ever since that time, singing for any audi-ence is only at request for a special, usually commemorative, event.

I decided that it should be a priority for me to seriously study English, because it is fundamental for adjusting to American life. Moreover, with improved language ability there could be greater opportunity to acquire a useful skill. Good thinking on my part. But a new family development was an immediate barrier. Bob was not entirely comfortable with Pentagon quasi-Army work. He managed to wrangle a contractor position with an assignment to Tehran, in Iran, as it was when governed by the royal ruler, the Shahanshah . . . the "king of kings."

We arrived in Tehran in September 1978, a tired assortment of six weary travelers. Our group comprised Bob, me, my mother, Catherine (almost six years old), Jaime (not yet two), and Victoria (just a four-month-old baby in arms). My two sons, Bao and Khai, stayed in Virginia at the Fairfax house with my father because they needed the consistency of remaining in the same school where orig-inally enrolled.

Descending from the plane, feeling the usual flight fatigue, com-plicated by travel with children, and immediately hearing a strange language all around, provided me with the same sense of awkward displacement that must have been how the average American had felt on entering Viet Nam. It was not only the language that was new to me, but more truly, in this new environment I was definitely the odd one, the foreigner . . . and I was feeling that way so much more deeply than when in Guam or Virginia. My mother and I had each other as anchors, and we would definitely focus on the children; but right away I felt it necessary to get some understanding of what was going on in this country where our family would live while Bob worked.

The natural way for me to enter, and attempt to understand, the Iranian environment would be simply getting out in the streets to shop for basic necessities. We needed bread, fresh vegetables, meat, and the local yogurt that we quickly learned to love. Although apprehensive at first, everything being totally new to me, I was soon exploring some parts of the city, at least those closest to where we lived. My mother and Cathy would sometimes be with me, but I often strolled alone. The streets were lively. Many were not vehicle throughways but instead narrow pedestrian alleys lined by merchant stalls. There was a dynamic bazaar atmosphere permeated by conversation in every shop. Fixed pricing would have been unimaginable for the vendors and accepted only by the naivest buyers. The Tehran market players were all realists and far from gullible. Bargaining was not only assumed but accepted as part of a discourse that was almost as much social as it was commercial.

Curious merchants, and sometimes eavesdropping customers, would almost always politely enquire as to my nationality. Their curiosity, as I experienced it, was never unfriendly, but when I asked people to guess, their range of replies was astonishing. Some thought, I know not why, that I might be Italian or Greek. A few would hesitatingly suggest my being Asian of exotic land. Only once did a young seller of textiles venture that I might be from Viet Nam! I think she was really surprised when my reply confirmed her guess. I would always find a way to mention that my husband was American, but—the ice having already been broken by casual conversation—the revelation of an American family connection never provoked hostility.

Artistic expression, whether by painting, carpet-making, or ceramics, is a conspicuous feature of Iranian culture. I was extraordinarily fascinated by woven textile floor coverings, perhaps because they are not part of our Vietnamese tradition. Exploring the maze of shops, observing local people handling a flat weave kilim or one of the thicker carpets, all distinctive by province, made me determined to learn more. After several days' inquiry, a friendly shopkeeper introduced me to a family that had a modest weaving enterprise employing women, almost all much younger than myself. Although I am a quick learner for arts (and much in construction), the rapidity with which experienced Persian fingers managed weft and warp was amazing to me. Soon I was able to work just as they did, although never with equivalent quickness. I worked up some designs on paper, and my new friends helped me with a small carpet. Later they even wove my floral images into some of their own work.

Learning from those friendly women allowed casual discovery, without intrusive questioning or an outsider's criticism, of what they believed were basic problems damaging their society and country. According to those new friends, not politically active but definitely observant, about a year before our family arrival, security forces working directly for the Shah confronted protesting demonstrators, killing and wounding several hundred. When I heard this story from the women around me, accompanied by much wincing and nodding, it seemed reasonable to compare their account to the 1963 Viet Nam tragedy in Hue when security forces killed several Buddhist demonstrators. But I could not imagine, and at first even doubted, the enormous difference in the number of fatalities. Several deaths in Hue, compared with several hundred in Tehran, stunned me. I was finally persuaded by the sincerity of the women that the Iran casualties were truly of that scale. How could it have happened?

I sought to understand by considering whether there was any parallel with Viet Nam's recent history. Gradually, and through conversations extending over three months, I was told that around thirty years earlier the Shah contended for primacy with a socialist/nationalistic political leader who led the Iran Parliament toward nationalizing foreign oil operations. Tension within Iran, and the involvement of foreign oil interests, persuaded the Shah to dismiss the prime minister. But that prime minister enjoyed some popular support, so the Shah himself had to depart for Europe. Incredibly, and probably much regretted today in light of subsequent developments, foreign intelligence services instigated a coup d'état to overthrow the popularly elected government and return the Shah from France to resume office as a royal dictator.

Now suppose, in my own country, that France could have succeeded in organizing a coup against Ngo Dinh Diem for the purpose of empowering Emperor Bao Dai in order to enhance French commercial interests. What would the Vietnamese reaction have been? Even if acknowledging subsequent errors by President Diem and the poor performance of follow-on military regimes, how much worse it would have been, how much more quickly the collapse of a noncommunist alternative, if the imperial power had reinstated bumbling emperor Bao Dai!

Within Iran, the restored Shah used unlimited power and secret police to enforce absolute loyalty. The consequences for even cautious dissent ranged from inhuman interrogation and prison to disappearance. Repression was so comprehensive that commercial, intellectual, and other modernizing political interests were rendered completely ineffective. Thus, the unintended result of foreign intrigue was that the only viable resistance to autocratic dictatorship became the Islamic religious movement, and Islam is so woven through Iranian society that energized religious leaders could not be intimidated. The mullahs became the opposition of last recourse for all who despised the Shah.

Now, due to our following Bob, I had inadvertently delivered Mother and my three young girls into the middle of another historic collapse. In December, street conflicts intensified. Once, Mother and I had to seek shelter in a friendly shop while Bob hid outside in our car as gunfire erupted nearby in broad daylight on the street. There were frequent demonstrations, with participants sometimes carrying the bodies of slain citizen martyrs. We lived on a hillside overlooking the city. Every night we would hear gunfire below, competing with echoing loudspeakers blaring over and over, "SHAHANSHAH ... SHAHANSHAH." Whether that was advocacy for support or call for overthrow, we never understood. Some soldiers mutinied and attacked government security units that were considered the backbone for the Shah maintaining his grip on power. The unravelling of his position accelerated toward the New Year of 1979.

Regime-dependent Iranian families, some government officials, wealthy persons, and foreign residents all hastened to make international flight reservations to escape an impending avalanche. We were no exception. The immediate problem for us was that every airline was swamped, seats were overbooked, and money purchased privileged access to the head of the line. Mother, my three daughters, and I were ticket holders for a January 15 departure. Bob delivered us to Mehrabad Airport but could not accompany us past security and into the departure area. On our own from that instant, we were gripped within a maelstrom of frantic humanity. Everyone, driven by fear-fueled energy, pushed themselves forward from long lines to checkpoints, to more long lines and then more checkpoints, each person moving forward in competition with other determined travelers.

Finally, we were outside on the tarmac, still in a tight competitive line but within sight of the wheeled boarding ramp, which looked to us like the stairway to heaven. We should ascend to the aircraft door, within which an attending steward made a final check of tickets and travel documents. We were so very close to salvation and, just then, right at the doorway, after some scrambling and conversation among crew members, we were informed that our seats had been sold, mysteriously, to others. Prompted by my loud angry protest, the ticket difficulty was resolved (I know not how) fairly quickly. But then we were informed the travel document for my mother was irregular, and she would have to stay.

Mother held an internationally recognized refugee travel document rather than a passport. Entry to Iran had been unquestioned, but now she was in danger of detention. I could not, and would not, allow that. She had saved me more than once when I was a child. Now, keeping a grip on all three of my daughters, I straddled the narrow gap where the stairway bridged to the aircraft door and resisted crew stewards trying to pull me within, while simultaneously shaking off a few would-be passengers who tried to pull me back down the stairs. I screamed that I would not move, and the airplane would not leave, without my mother. Children crying, and Mother nearly fainting, the standoff persisted for almost an hour until at last, a determined American diplomatic officer arrived from the embassy and explained our documentation once again to Mehrabad officials and airplane crew. We were finally allowed to board, together, and then held our breath until lifting off the runway. I knew how Vietnamese had felt in 1975 when thousands sought escape and safety by any means.

We arrived in France at Charles de Gaulle Airport the same day, caught our connecting flight a few hours later, and on January 16, 1979, landed in New York. The Shah, "king of kings," fled his country a second time, and on this occasion his departure would be permanent.

We returned to Virginia and the house in Fairfax that was maintained by my father while sons Bao and Khai were continuing their schooling. Bob very soon followed us to Virginia because American commercial operations—in fact foreign contracting of any sort— were no longer viable in Tehran. Bob moped around the house for a bit until he was able to resume a position connected to the Pentagon. Once again, he would proceed each morning, uniformed, to some vague clerical job, sort of quasi-military. I recall that his jacket insignia included a RANGER badge, although he seemed distinctly non-ranger to me. Still, he maintained the appearance, and received the pay, of someone whose duties must have represented some value for national defense.

Within our home—that house purchased with assistance from the sale of some of Mother's jewelry to help Bob put together the down payment—we all played our extended-family roles. Mother and Father, but especially Mother, supported Bob by serving as domestic help. I was, naturally, principally responsible for all the children, preparing Bao, Khai (renamed David and Anthony for ease of assimilation), and Catherine for school each day. Then, once they were out the front door, I would turn my attention to Jaime and Vickie respectively about two years and one year of age. Bob never involved himself with childcare, never changed even one diaper, never fed the infants. I bless my mother, every day remembering her, for all the help that she gave me and, through me, each of our children.

Bob was not satisfied with being one of the anonymous Pentagon commuter soldiers. Remembering the higher remuneration and comfortable lifestyle of a Saigon contractor, then surveying construction and property activity in Maryland and Virginia, he decided to form a company for remodeling and construction. He planned to begin modestly and, if successful, expand as opportunity allowed. I suppose it was for tax purposes and to satisfy the appearance of Pentagon propriety that he prepared required legal paperwork describing me as the enterprise owner and director.

Bob soon relied on me to locate and temporarily hire, job by job, Vietnamese refugees as company laborers. Some projects brought our work team to tough neighborhoods within the Washington district proper. I would go with them to provide reassurance and insulation from occasional unfriendly residents who were not used to having Asians on their street. So doing, I learned by direct exposure—and practice in providing persuasive explanation—something about the tension between owners of the properties being upgraded and tenants renting that property. The owners wanted to pay our company as little as possible, then increase the rent as much as possible when making new agreements with tenants.

Sometimes there would be a lag between our completion of contractual work and payment by the property owner. That gap would leave us short of cash to pay our workers, requiring me to beg for their understanding, and in a few instances my mother was asked again to provide a little money to cover the deficit. Month after month, Bob would continue to present me with papers to sign, with nothing completely, or even generally, explained.

The housing market was so active, with rising prices for home purchase and rental, that Bob overextended on credit to take ownership of a condo project in his home state of Pennsylvania. But when banks later became cautious, he had to sell that property with my signature necessarily applied once again. Gradually, driven by gratitude for his having delivered my family to American sanctuary, I began working full time for the construction company. Now more than just signing paperwork and collecting money due the company, I acquired basic skills for installing tiles, roofing, and drywall. My two boys, when not in school, were also pressed into service for heavy work. We carried packs of shingles, navigating ladders even up to condominium roofs. We worked through filthy crawl spaces beneath old buildings. Although doing the part-time labor of adults, the boys were not paid wages. Pocket money and the character-building benefit of work discipline had to suffice as compensation.

The same applied to me. I was not salaried, simply given an occasional allowance, most of which I had to apply against household expenses. Completely dependent on my husband for explanations, I was not even aware there should have been a company record of salaries with mandated deductions. I was ignorant of the requirement to document and provide for social security. I would always sign whatever paperwork, including licensing a second company, that Bob placed before me. With my limited knowledge of English, to this day I do not understand how he handled financial reporting and tax liabilities.

Thinking back to those years, I fear there may have been some fiddling, misrepresentation, and lack of compliance with social security and tax laws. Perhaps I was reported as salaried when I was not. My mother and father may have been reported as dependents when they were not; there is no way for me to know. Mother and Father, as unpaid domestic staff, were miserable. Informed by a friend about alternative living options, they escaped to senior housing. Now I felt isolated, very lonely, stressed by work and home circumstances, comforted only by the children.

Each day I would visit the sites where our company had a project, ensure there were no problems, check on the morale of the workers, and emphasize that even while sticking to a schedule, quality should never be compromised. If there was just one project under way, I would stay at that location and work as if one of the laborers. When we were short a worker who could handle heavy loads, I would necessarily step into the breach. As a result, to this day I suffer from severe spinal damage. Near-constant pain is the reminder of my sacrifice for others, especially my three Viet Nam children. Sometimes, when Mother and Father could not watch the preschoolers, Jamie and Vickie would have to come with me. It was not easy to keep an eye on them and supervise projects and workers. Often, I would be tasked with a special part of the work, usually either tiling or the final decorative touches. I was pretty good at tile work, and in fact when Bob promised the widow of a friend to redo her flooring, he brought me to her house and they both watched while I did as he had promised.

I was fair with all the workers, and sometimes even loaned them small amounts from my own allowance. Once when we were desperately short meeting a payroll, my mother stepped forward again to provide money from the sale of her jewelry, baubles that I had accumulated when a popular entertainer many years past in Saigon. Bob always expressed appreciation, but he never repaid her, even years later when she was hospitalized. When I asked on that occasion, he replied that since three years had passed there was no obligation for him to repay.

I encouraged one of the young Americans to get himself back into school part-time. He became a sort of stepson, was occasionally helpful around the house, and sometimes accompanied me when bringing the children to Chuck E. Cheese or to a park with slides and swings. He had sort of a mild crush on me, despite quite an age difference, and that irritated Bob. However, after he once fixed Bob's car, the potential unfounded jealousy seemed to diminish.

As months, and then a few years, passed, Bob seemed satisfied if I saw to his companies while he watched football games on television. He usually greeted me at our door, when I wearily returned, with a clumsy impromptu belly dance while holding an opened can of beer. Although I would be aching to the bone, wanting nothing more than a bath and sleep, he too often insisted on exercising the passion that he always insisted was for me and me alone.

But then one evening, following more than a full day of work at one of our projects, I stopped on the way home for a drink with two of our workers in the public lounge of the Key Bridge Marriott Hotel. And guess what? Bob was right there with the widow whose floors I had tiled. Their appearance together was more than just convivial. My sixth sense activated, and I was sure that their date was not the first. I tipped our waiter to bring refresher drinks to "Mr. Henry and Friend," from "Mrs. Henry."

Later, after returning home, I was attacked. Bob had been waiting behind the door, and he struck me so hard that I was knocked to the floor. Then he straddled my back and beat on me until pushed away by the young American worker who had accompanied me to the house, just because I feared exactly that kind of situation. The police were called. Before they arrived, Bob pricked his finger slightly with a knife, squeezed drops of blood onto his shirt, and claimed that I had attacked him. The police were not convinced, and I doubt my sons ever believed his story. The next day, when I was interviewed in the hospital, the police urged me to make a statement that would allow them to bring charges and make an arrest. I felt that I had better not.

The interviewing officers warned me that a first instance of abuse was often followed by an escalation of brutal behavior. I was definitely afraid that Bob might beat me again and that the first act of physical violence could become habitual. But, like many, perhaps most, women in my situation, I rationalized the unacceptable: maybe I could have dealt with circumstances differently. Although not my fault, and I absolutely should not have been beaten, maybe I could have moderated Bob's anger had I tried an approach other than sarcasm.

And, more important, probably just like other mothers, I worried what might happen if Bob were to be arrested. Would his security clearance for Pentagon employment be revoked? Would he lose his job? What would be the impact on his own parents, or for our children? Would I be blamed by Bob's parents and siblings, or even by my own children? How could I manage the home mortgage payments and all the other paperwork that Bob always handled?

So, I suffered the situation, carried on with heavy heart, endured. But I knew without doubt that, as necessary as it had been to depart Viet Nam, and later to escape from Tehran, someday I would have to leave this oppressive and now abusive marriage. I worried about the children. Bao had completed college, with my allowing Bob to sell one of my diamonds to pay the final year's tuition and fees. Khai was close to finishing his degree. I believed Bob would do well by the three girls because they were of his blood. My mother and father were living independently.

Eventually I told Bob that I would leave, and that he should understand that my departure was the beginning of our separation. With lighter heart, even though completely lacking any plan, I went out the door.

I was, as though fired from a cannon, exactly like an explosive round of high velocity, but human in composition, encountering drag, slipping off target, decelerating, lacking direction, tumbling, and striking the intervening unintended. My name could have been Ricochet.

With almost empty pockets, I fled far westward. Why California? Well, it was about as distant as possible from Virginia and there were Vietnamese Americans in large numbers clustered around San Jose and farther south in Orange County. I chose Orange County, naively, for having always liked oranges. A blind but good choice, with a few acquaintances of past Viet Nam days already there. Extensive tropical fruit groves were a distant memory, but almost every home still had a small garden.

My first attempt at opening an independent business—barely on a shoestring, and in an effort to replicate the Guam experience—was to establish a clothing enterprise. KV Fashion was immediately successful. The demand was insistent, especially on the part of Vietnamese women, years after their arrival in America and now wanting to dress with style. My name was well known by those familiar with my past film roles, and I think some purchases were made simply because people wanted to let their friends know that a given dress had been purchased from me. I had one major difficulty: a continuing lack of English-language skills. Oh, I could converse with customers, but the intricacy of local government regulations, billing and accounting, and state and local tax practice just overwhelmed me.

I was rescued by Tran Van Thanh, the young son of General Tran Van Don, erstwhile beneficiary of the 1963 coup and murder of President Diem. The younger Tran male had followed me in

Dalat like a puppy, much more innocent than his father. Now he appeared in California, offering to take on the bookkeeping of my business. There was a catch, however. He rather deftly handled the management and billing, but his tastes were expensive, especially as regards frequent air travel and personal long-distance phone calls, all paid by my company.

The tipping point was a local California earthquake on October 1, 1987. The center was in Whittier, but the impact extended to Bellflower, where we had our manufacturing facility and office. I was frightened; that was enough California for me, at least right then. The thorough shaking I received might have also carried a subliminal message: "Get back to Virginia and finish what you started; get a divorce." Unofficial, or even legal, separation, was not enough for me. I needed a divorce for true freedom.

The marriage, for me, had been from the beginning *sans passion*, and the divorce, on my part, was *sans haine*. Bob, true to his nature, was a bit devious, insisting that we use the lawyers he retained in order to smooth the process. Supposing I would claim an interest in the house, Bob had already taken out a second mortgage on the property and squirreled that money away. He assumed I would want to take our guest table settings and collector's items, so he removed those and hid them at a house belonging to one of his friends. He told one of my sons that I had taken all the plates and dishes. Feeling sorry for him, my son purchased a replacement set of tableware for Bob. But later, after our divorce, when he brought the originals back, his cheap trickery was revealed.

As to the house, bank accounts, and all else, I made no claim despite friends suggesting that at least some part of the joint marital property should be mine. I thought instead that Bob Henry could be a stable platform, with no encumbrances while he shouldered the responsibility for raising daughters Cathy, Jaime, and Victoria. I just wanted to be away and free. There was a lot of back and forth between the lawyers and Bob. The transactions were either entirely over my head or behind my back. In the end, the bottom line—and not just literally, as in where a divorce document is signed—was that I was again virtually penniless, but free. What to do now?

CHAPTER 14

Relativity

T ime is truly relative. Of course, we know that units for measuring time are absolute: sixty seconds per minute, sixty minutes per hour, and so on. But we learn that measuring phenomena depends on the relationship between observer and observed, and even the act of measuring can affect what is measured. This is especially so with respect to the passage of time while you are within its flow. When we are four to five years old, most of us establish a recollection platform on which we begin to accumulate memories of all we experience or have been taught. In later years, when our brain is tasked to function as a search engine, a specific memory may be difficult to retrieve from our "personal library" stacks. Frustrating!

But as to the relativity of time observed: when we are seven years old, as I was in 1946 in Tra Vinh, one year represents a very high percentage of life lived since hitting that age-five platform for memory recall. After all, the year from age six to seven is fifty percent of the life lived since the memory base established at age five. Conversely, one year at age fifty is little more than two percent of your life lived since age five. So, within that fiftieth year, or a season of that year, time really does seem to "fly by."

My final entries then, even while spanning as many years as did the first twelve chapters, will be brief, because for me time seemed to flow more quickly and with surprising turbulence. Having been an entertainer in Viet Nam—often compared to Sophia Loren by Saigon writers, and later receiving the national award for best actress from President Thieu; I can share a piece of cinematic history with you. Little more than a hundred years ago, "The Perils of Pauline" was an American film serial of many weekly installments within which the lead actress would continually cope with uncomfortable and distressing circumstances, to finally survive at the end because of her own courage and resourcefulness. I frequently felt as though I was a bit like the cinematic Pauline, living within a script of my own troubled life.

The divorce from Bob was finally complete, and I was free but lacking any sea anchor. Tran Van Thanh, just recently a functional partner in my pre-earthquake clothing enterprise, suggested, and then began insisting, that solution to the problem of my destitute life might be marriage with him. He was eight years my junior and had worshipped me in Dalat when a student. Now it was as though he believed a juvenile dream could come true.

Bob Henry's motivation in marrying me had been to prove his manhood and acquire stature by capturing the most popular actress and singer of the sybaritic wartime Saigon scene. Of course, for me the sole intention had been to save my family. On both our parts there was an insufficiency of glue for a good long life together. So, when Thanh became a supplicant, I wondered about his reasons. I thought that part of Thanh's compulsion might be a desire to prove himself by marriage to the one woman that his father—bumbling, egotistical, murderous General Tran Van Don—could not bed.

Did I ever think about Frank, that green-eyed sometimes haunt of my dreams? My mother wondered, and even more than once asked me. Well, yes, I occasionally did. He was probably in a remote part of some far-away country. I never sought to enquire. I did not want to see him again, even though I could not entirely forget him.

Thanh and I conversed at length, on several occasions. He had really helped me in California, but now we were in Virginia, and he was unemployed. I finally agreed that we could marry, so long as he understood that the relationship would be for mutual support and not love. He was satisfied, I think, with at least a partial attainment of his dream and hoped that time together would deepen affection. He had known, those many years earlier in Dalat, that I loved Frank, but now I told Thanh to refrain from ever mentioning that name. We married in mid-April 1988 and, because young Thanh was unemployed, we lived temporarily with his parents, the Andre Tran Van Dons.

The Tran Van Don family (and I make the reference to "Andre" because that was his French name) considered themselves aristocrats among Vietnamese exiles in America. Don had been born in France and had trained and served in the French army, all before he joined the South Viet Nam army, ingratiated himself with President Diem, and later positioned himself as a leader of the 1963 military coup that concluded with murdering the president. Now in Virginia, the family would hold frequent dining-room table meetings, presided over by the former general, always very focused on the distinctly fine social reputation of their branch of the Tran family. I, a more modest child of the South, rarely attended, so I was sometimes criticized by the treacherous patriarch and his wife. I would always respond that as a simple member of the extensive Nguyen family, akin to an everywhere-everyday common citizen, there was nothing for me to say. I felt a sense of suffocation in that house. Something had to be done.

The "something" consisted of helping Thanh obtain a position with the World Bank. His refugee status had provided him with Canadian citizenship based on having studied there during the Viet Nam War. Now he could apply for employment, as a Canadian citizen, at the World Bank headquarters on H Street in Washington, DC. I knew a senior officer in that organization and arranged for

Thanh to have an interview. I expected that he would be working in the Washington office, and we would live independently in Virginia.

Surprise! Thanh was accepted for a World Bank position, but with a posting to Africa! Onward to another eye-opening adventure. I use this term because it is part of our very human nature to believe we know much about a place even if we have never been there. Ask anyone in another country about Australia, and that person will be pretty sure they "know a bit" about kangaroos, the outback, and beaches. On arriving in Australia, however, a traveler will be surprised at how little had been truly known and understood. This applies even more emphatically to travel within and between countries of an entire continent. I found that each African country is specific to itself and differs considerably from its neighbors. "Africans" are no more generic than "Asians."

Thanh took his first assignment in the Republic of Côte d'Ivoire in 1991. As the name suggests, that country was once a possession of France. In fact, the one point of commonality on the continent is that most of Africa was previously seized and ruled by various European countries in the mad imperial scramble for rule over other peoples that characterized the eighteenth and nineteenth centuries. In Africa the rivals were chiefly Belgium, England, France, Portugal, and the marvelous (when at home in their own country) Dutch. One can still see residual evidence of which European country ruled in a part of Africa by what European language was later adopted for convenient international use.

Mother was not as healthy and resilient, having suffered occasional illness, as she had been a few years earlier. My concern was sufficient to cause me to suggest that I stay and care for her, but Thanh insisted that he would need me while making the transition from new World Bank employee to a foreign posting valued team member. So, believing that the assignment away from Washington would be about three years, with an opportunity for home leave, I told mother that my absence would not be for long

I was surprised, and occasionally made uncomfortable, by the World Bank and foreign diplomatic mission lifestyle, an ostentatious level of comfort compared with that of local populations in Abidjan and other African cities. These were places that, sometimes for years in a few countries, suffered civil strife ranging from internal political warfare to sectarian violence. Crime was pervasive. Corruption was endemic. Citizens lived with uncertainty and apprehension of danger all around.

But diplomats, and especially World Bank representatives, lived much like the colonial-imperialists who preceded them before African countries achieved independence. In fact, by taking over palatial colonial homes, the internationalists risked appearing like a new breed of foreign master. We lived (with a feeling of guilt, on my part) in a grand home rented by the World Bank. We had servants and guards on the property. We were popular host and hostess within the foreign community, including a small cluster of Vietnamese in Abidjan centered on a restaurant operated by the former South Viet Nam ambassador who had remained in Côte d'Ivoire after 1975.

My most serious personal difficulty was derivative of Thanh being a good son, a better man than his father. Tran Van Don, who once strode the Viet Nam stage as an army general officer, maker of coup, and the last (for a few 1975 days) defense minister of the Republic of Viet Nam, inserted himself into our lives. He had been progressively estranged from other family members and commensurably depressed, and so reached out to Thanh. My young husband, and in truth having no real alternative, responded positively by inviting his father to come live with us in Abidjan. That aging patriarch too soon began to assume a baronial role in our home. He would suggest to Thanh a social schedule for the month and adopt the manner of host with our guests.

Once, while Thanh was absent on travel to nearby Nigeria, old Don even made an amorous advance upon me, an error promptly corrected by my throwing him to the floor so violently that he was bloodied and could rise only with the assistance of two servants. When Thanh returned, the old goat told his son that it had been I who flirted with him! Of course, Thanh believed me, but he—or rather, we—were stuck with Don because nobody else would take him.

In part as consolation, and perhaps also because Thanh feared that I might be the one to leave, we began to travel together more frequently. We even brought my three youngest daughters, Cathy, Jaime, and Victoria, on a vacation to France, Italy, and Spain. All transportation costs were covered by the World Bank, making me wonder again, even as I was enjoying the advantages, whether international organizations were always mission focused.

A short visit to Egypt was overwhelming from an entirely different perspective. I am Roman Catholic, pretty much to the core, but also a person who believes that an evolutionary process occurred on our planet. That does leave open the question of whether a deity ignited the process, with or without intelligent design. But regardless of that deeper query, I do accept evidence that humans diverged from other primate species in Africa, evolved in developing speech and tool use, and began a drift toward the Mediterranean, the Levant, and even further. Even so, standing before the pyramids bewildered my brain.

Yes, pyramids and tombs for dictatorial royal rulers may have been built on the backs of slaves, as were later grand public works of Greece and Rome. But even so, any observer must absolutely acknowledge the quantum leap that was made from simple Paleolithic stone implements to Mediterranean engineering, mathematics, and written records. Angkor of Cambodia was magnificent but died in the jungle; the image and enduring significance of pyramids lives on today. Just take a look at our dollar bill and the Great Seal of the United States.

Thanh knew that aching memories of our birth country, Viet Nam, were always in my heart. So, he suggested as an antidote to the tension, slowly growing between us—a consequence of prolonged distance from my mother while having to cope with his presumptuous old father—a trip back to Viet Nam! We had visited briefly in 1991, traveling as a family on his laissez-passer. There was no difficulty with police. Particularly pleasant was being able to visit with best friend Kim Chi, but entirely depressing was witnessing the poverty, especially on the part of street urchins who seemed to be everywhere scrambling for scraps of anything.

Now we received a visa from the Viet Nam embassy in Paris and arrived at Tan Son Nhut Airport on November 11, 1993. The atmosphere was noticeably different from that during the visit only two years earlier. Viet Nam–American relations were slowly improving. In 1991, a field office for American MIA operations was established in Hanoi. Early the next year an American ban against travel to Viet Nam was lifted, and consequently both countries had already opened a liaison office in each other's capital prior to our 1993 return to Saigon.

On arrival it was apparent that our visit, entirely personal on our part but coordinated by a semiofficial organization for reconciliation (referred to as Hai Ngoai Dan Toc), would be considered part of the overall warming trend. A protocol officer at the airport introduced himself by saying that he would be assisting with reservations for travel, including a flight to Hanoi, and arrangements for meetings. When we expressed surprise, he responded that the government welcomed my return as an important cultural figure. Puzzling.

The Saigon environment seemed improved. Economic reform policies appeared to be having a positive effect. We found people were completely open in greeting American travelers. Two years earlier we had taken a meal at the small restaurant operated by Madame Nguyen Phuoc Dai, and now we returned there again. She had been a prominent lawyer and elected senator during the time of the Republic of Viet Nam but in 1975 chose to remain in Saigon even though many of her family members left the country. There were some who supposed that her decision proved she was a secret communist. I felt otherwise.

I had first met her decades earlier during the presidency of Ngo Dinh Diem when she ingratiated herself with Tran Le Xuan (the rather infamous Madame Nhu); joined the Ngo family-sponsored Women's Solidarity Movement; and was granted a seat in the National Assembly. During the second Republic of Viet Nam, she was elected to the senate as an "opposition candidate." I thought her a charming opportunist, someone who had supposed the communists would honor her "progressive" record. But instead of being rewarded after 1975, she was basically ignored as irrelevant. When learning that we were invited to meet with officials in Hanoi she asked to accompany us. I did not have any objection, and neither did the helpful protocol officer.

We made a side trip to Dalat, where I controlled my tears while remembering past happiness, and then moved by air onward to Hanoi. This northern city was of less interest for me because I lacked any previous association with its people and places.

There were actually three protocol meetings arranged for us. One was with Do Muoi, at the time general secretary of the Communist Party. He enquired whether I would consider returning to and living in Viet Nam, so as to contribute to cultural enrichment and promote the national cinema. My rehearsed response, having anticipated the question, was that I was committed to life in America because my children were all living there. He nodded, as if my reply was reasonable, then asked whether I might have any query for him.

Yes, I did. I told him that everywhere in Viet Nam there seemed to be many more Chinese, and patently Chinese businesses, than before. I suggested that for any Viet Nam government the most persistent issue will always be maintaining independence from China. What would the government of Viet Nam, given the border war several years earlier, do to preserve national independence considering the hundreds of years of contention and China's recent assertiveness?

Do Muoi hesitated, leaned back, and finally responded that I was raising old history, and that in a new era Viet Nam and China would cooperate to resolve any small issues.

I was skeptical.

Do Muoi seemed mystified by Nguyen Phuoc Dai's attendance and, curious, asked an aide about her. After receiving a whispered explanation, he asked whether the lady had anything to share. Madame Dai had previously asked me to raise the matter of reopening her attorney's office, and I had told her that she should address the issue herself. Now she had an opportunity to explain that she had encountered some difficulty in obtaining permission to open an office for her legal work. Do Muoi told one of his aides to look into that matter. Our meeting concluded.

My personal impression is that Do Muoi was a completely serious, almost morose, man. When I first set my recollections on paper, he was still alive, over one hundred years of age, and died only in 2018. I wonder if he was then still convinced of China as a good neighbor, with only good intentions.

Another meeting was with Prime Minister Vo Van Kiet. Although they were partners in intrigue, and tough operators, Vo Van Kiet seemed more personable than Do Muoi. Perhaps I had that impression because we were both displaced southerners, me to North America and he to North Viet Nam.

Vo Van Kiet was born in the southern province of Vinh Long, and most of his personal history with the Communist Party was in the south, whereas Do Muoi was born in the north and spoke the relatively harsh inflection of that dialect, wherein our softer sibilant "sh" becomes a buzzing "s" and our soft "y" becomes a sharper "z." Life experience and postwar responsibility governing in the south seemed to have inclined Vo Van Kiet to advocate the more flexible economy that was adopted as policy and cautiously put into practice beginning in the late 1980s.

Our third meeting was with Phan Van Khai, who like Vo Van Kiet was by origin a southerner (from the Cu Chi District northwest of Saigon). Khai was also part of the Vo Van Kiet "economic reform-ist" movement within the Communist Party and was equally per-sonable. Phan Van Khai eventually became prime minister and, like Do Muoi, died in 2018.

Thanh expected that my appreciation for being able to travel within our birth country would ease the tension between us, but his stupidity in carrying out a chore on behalf of his father, without tell-ing me, almost resulted in his arrest. As it was, he was detained and questioned for several hours. The evening after our meeting with Party leaders, there had been a note waiting at our hotel informing Thanh that he would be picked up the next morning for a discus-sion at one of the national security offices. When I asked what that note really meant, Thanh responded that it might be in connection with the letters that he had carried and delivered for his father. How naive he had been, and how angry I was! When I asked why he had not told me, he responded that he had not thought it important.

The next morning, I went shopping in narrow bustling Hanoi streets. Long after I returned to the hotel, Thanh still had not reap-peared. When I found our escort/protocol officer standing by a counter, he told me that Thanh had been taken away to a security/ police office, and a note was left for me providing the address. I went there immediately. The officer in charge introduced himself as Mr. Huyet (translatable as "blood," so definitely not auspicious) and he met with me in the hallway while Thanh remained inside an office. When I asked why Thanh had been brought there, I was politely but somewhat glibly informed that Thanh had not been arrested, only sought out because he was a cultured gentleman and spoke such sophisticated French that it was a pleasure to converse with him. Several hours had already passed. I called the Hai Ngoai Dan Toc office to complain and then, still angry, told Mr. Huyet that I was in Hanoi for meetings with senior leaders, including Do Muoi, and the detention of my husband was not at all in accordance with the intent and spirit of our visit. Moreover, if Thanh were not released,

I would immediately complain to those senior leaders. The response was that of course Thanh was not arrested, and any inconvenience was unintentional.

Within a short time, Thanh was allowed to depart the premises with me. I was relieved, but furious. If this situation had occurred only a few years earlier he, and perhaps I as well, would certainly have been arrested. As it was, the next day at the Hanoi airport he was detained for "further discussion," and our aircraft departure was delayed until I descended and strenuously complained. I was aggravated, but on reflection understood that on this occasion we really had been treated delicately (relative to past years) because the United States and Viet Nam were cautiously working toward normalizing relations for trade and diplomatic representation. Hanoi did not want to "rock the boat."

We returned to Africa, but our continual strained relationship was no bond for stability in a marriage lacking love. Learning that Mother was ill and feeling guilty for having been away for much longer than I really should have been, I flew back to Virginia. We had only a few days together before hospitalization was necessary. Intubated, she could no longer speak. Communicating only through her eyes, she seemed to have so much regret.

Mother died, and I felt like a part of me had gone up and away with her. I returned to Abidjan, but the reunion with Thanh was not happy for either of us. After several months, I packed lightly, leaving most of my clothing, jewelry, and even some money behind. I wrote a letter for Thanh, telling him that we both needed space and time to reconsider our futures, and that I would begin by flying back to America. I did not tell him that my destination would be California.

My first child, daughter Le Thu, was still in Orange County. We reconnected and resumed collaboration in a modest dry-cleaning and alterations business, with some retail sales. I was content to spend time with her and otherwise be alone. We occasionally went out to restaurants together and one evening joined a holiday reception at the Hilton hotel in Huntington Beach. It was a festive occasion, and almost every table was full. A gentleman, distinguished by wearing a tuxedo, approached. At first I thought he might be a hotel employee. But he was in fact another guest, looking for a place to roost. He asked whether there might be space at our table. There was, and my daughter invited him to take the chair between us. He was courteous and personable, easy to converse with on the first meeting. Other ladies at the table thought him intriguing, but I was the one he asked to see again.

I wanted companionship without the emotional commitment. He surely wanted more, but despite what he may have told friends and family members, I was never other than a very good friend. I did do some work for him. He was preparing a house for sale and asked me to "spruce the place up," making it more attractive in what was then in a sizzling real estate market. I did that for him, and when the property sold for more than he expected, he provided me with a commission.

Kenneth Gunn was a prominent businessman in Orange County. He owned, he told me, three businesses. The most active one was for maintenance and rental of massive construction equipment. He also owned multiple rental properties in California and elsewhere. He had a boat, not quite a yacht but grander than a runabout. Ken moved smoothly within the wealthy Newport Beach-to-Huntington Beach circles. We socialized at parties and restaurants with his friends and four adult children from previous marriages, his spouses having predeceased him. We were comfortable with each other. Regrettably, his health began to decline following a stroke that occurred when his car was struck by another vehicle. He was hospitalized, then released for return home.

I was already scheduled for travel to Virginia to visit my children. Ken told me to go ahead, that he would be fine, and we could speak by telephone for mutual reassurance. That worked for a few days, but then one evening he seemed confused on the phone, complaining about people in the room with him. Gradually I understood that two other people had beds in the same room; as he struggled to describe the surroundings, it was obvious that he was not in his own house. I guessed that he had been placed in a nursing home of some kind and the next day flew back to California.

Exactly as I had supposed, Ken had been moved to an assisted-living facility. The conditions were on the lower end of any objective scale. The room was not as clean as it should have been. Some of his clothes, brought with him on the presumption of a long-term stay, were missing. Most critically, Ken was extremely unhappy. I resolved, and promised Ken, to bring him back to his own house and to arrange for continuing home care. The situation was grim and disturbing for me personally, as I imagined my own feelings if placed by family members in a similar situation.

The manager of the care facility surprised me, and Ken's children, by informing us that Ken had made a power of attorney for health care, naming me as the person to make decisions on his behalf. He remained in the care facility for about two weeks while his children reached an agreement for his return home. The manager kindly assisted me in locating a home-care professional to assist Ken in his own house. We tried a few until we found one that Ken was comfortable with in terms of handling personal hygiene needs and moving unobtrusively around the house. Our choice, Manny, was a young male nurse from the Philippines who was strong enough to lift Ken when he fell, move him to and from bed, and place him securely in his wheelchair.

Ken believed that my holding power of attorney for his health care would be strengthened if my separation from Thanh was made legally conclusive. I did not think such clarification would have much bearing on the home health care that I managed on Ken's behalf. But since I knew in my heart that Thanh and I would never again be under the same roof, it just made sense to finalize our break. So, with the assistance of lawyers, a day in June 1996 was determined to be the legal date of separation, and our divorce was decreed final on July 11, 2000.

We were in a small restaurant with his son and a daughter one evening when Ken suddenly had difficulty speaking, could not express his thoughts, and experienced a sort of stiffening on one side of his body that made movement awkward. We took him to a hospital where he seemed to stabilize but functioned at a lower plateau. He had suffered a second stroke. Even so, he continued to believe that he would be able to cope at home with the assistance of physicians, whom he saw on a regular basis, and Manny and me. But from that point onward, Ken took a slow downward turn.

He repeatedly tried to execute papers that would provide me with a small percentage of his primary business, and I just as consistently refused, telling him that it was his family business, I was exterior to the family, and all the business owners should be his children. Eventually I agreed to be beneficiary on a life insurance policy, and per his will and testament accept the house to which I had brought him home, after rescuing him from the three-to-a-room nursing facility. Those two points established, Ken began to insist that we marry . . . to protect me, he said.

I was finally persuaded, and so with a friend as witness we were married in an Orange County Court civil ceremony on February 15, 2005. As a continuing consequence of the strokes, Ken required assistance to stand. The explanation of steps in the civil marriage process needed repetition. The administering clerk of court made sure that Ken was acting of his own free will and that Ken understood he was entering into a state of marriage and desired to do so.

Almost a year and a half later, Ken died on July 26, 2006. There was an immediate clash with his four adult children who, led by his son and namesake, moved to assert themselves as sole beneficiaries. I doubt that money alone is root of all evil. There are other contenders for consideration: ambition regardless of consequence, excessive attachment to the desirable, envy of other people, and more. But it does seem to me that money is the primary fuel for explosive litigation.

Eventually, and it was a long eventuality, beginning late in 2007, eighteen months after Ken's death, there was movement toward a final settlement in order to eliminate emotional trauma and cut the continuing cost of litigation. The prolonged wrangling was emotionally painful for all parties. Afterward, and continuing through today, I am so relieved of the tension that I truly wish Kenneth Gunn's son and three daughters health, happiness, and extraordinary business success.

When Ken was alive, persons supposing that he was wealthier than was actually the case would solicit us for financial assistance, always posited as an "investment opportunity." One of those was Huynh Dao Nghia, also known as "Bruno," who had been a successful Maxim's restauranteur in Saigon in decades past. He approached us in early 2004 with a proposal for investment in a mixed upscale/fast food enterprise in South China. We were, foolishly, persuaded, and lost fifty thousand dollars—purloined by said Bruno, who provided a portion to his girlfriend.

Now, alone again, I was targeted by people, even by some I thought could be trusted, who believed me an easy mark for loans that would never need repayment. And fool that I was, this happened more than once. The illusion of my "wealth," although I was not as rich as people supposed, apparently allowed others to consider me legitimate prey.

My most painful disagreement of that period was with my daughter Jaime. She had been more than helpful—indispensable, in fact—during the litigation that followed Ken's death. She located the lawyer who represented me and provided a daughter's emotional support over the course of two stressful years. I always told her that in appreciation, I would provide her with a share of the settlement. Now she rather abruptly insisted on an immediate fifty thousand dollars to promote her singing career. The settlement, particularly the insurance policy money, had yet to be disbursed. If she had been patient a few more days, the money would have been hers, but she had made up her mind to push me right away. We parted with some bitterness that I will always regret.

But I have learned that no relationship is extinguished so long as both parties live; thus, I believe that someday we shall reconcile. I look forward to that reunion.

EPILOGUE
Odds and Ends

You may be thinking that the epilogue subtitle sums up my life story as having been an odd one, now that you have almost reached the end. But what I have in mind as "odds and ends" is a remembrance of working with fabrics. Beginning in Guam, and later in California, I have designed clothes for myself and friends, and occasionally for the market. Even today I retain five sewing machines, each with a different capability. Design and sewing will test a seamstress's ability, and a special skill is required to avoid waste by using remnant odds and ends to fashion something useful. So it is with my life, collecting and stitching together experiences and feelings to share with you.

Vietnamese living in America frequently ask me who among my contemporaries were my favorite actresses and singers, and how do I compare myself with those I admire? Any one of us would probably respond differently, because it is such a subjective question. Your very answer is dependent on who you are and how you see yourself within the artistic environment of a certain time and place.

Well, anyway, I always reply that these singers and songs are, for me, extraordinary: Thai Thanh, born in Hanoi and a few years older than I, established the highest bar against which all the rest of us are measured. Of all those whom I knew well, she with the sweetest voice was Bach Yen. Khanh Ly sang with unmatched passionate energy, and Thanh Thuy will always resonate with me for her version of the haunting melody "Chieu Mua Bien Gioi," wherein a woman sings of rain on the border while wondering where her soldier has gone. "Biet Kinh Ky" can be understood as a soldier's response, calling on his friends to fill their glasses and toast the following day, when he will be gone far away. The musician and sometimes painter Trinh Cong Son offered songs that even today bond people of the three Viet Nam regions. His paintings, on the lines of "finger painting," are scarce. I wish that I still had one.

When occasionally asked about American songs and the artists who sang them, I always smile, attached as I am to Orange County in California, not far from that Huntington Beach enclave calling itself "Surf City," so my response must be . . . the Beach Boys! That admission really dates me as an American senior citizen, but their musical pulsation, not unlike waves rolling on the beach where they once surfed, and their unique California phrasing, is insistently infectious and, once heard, is unforgettable.

As to Viet Nam cinema and film actresses, Tham Thuy Hang has a sweetness of character that permeates all her screen roles. She has been consistently generous when working with others, and I always felt we had a warm, mutually supportive relationship off screen as well as within film. I think that Kieu Chinh is a miraculous craftswoman who easily moves from role to role as required by any script. She began working in films while I was still a student and civic action cadre. My first roles were usually small supporting ones, but Kieu Chinh was a star from the "get go." No Vietnamese actress has appeared in more films, international as well as national. She is a promotional genius, and in a different postwar Viet Nam would eventually have become a major director and producer.

My life experience was different in some respects. Participating in civic action missions just as the Republic of Viet Nam established itself in the mid-1950s stimulated in me a love of country that ener-gized my few film roles. While Tham Thuy Hang and Kieu Chinh were born in the North and spoke with that sophisticated dialect, I was a child of the South and, even when working from a script, could not shake my southern accent. There were singers who did not appear in film, and actresses who did not sing, but I succeeded at both. I was not better than the others, but I was definitely differ-ent from most. My preference, I candidly reveal to you, was singing. Giving voice to convey emotion was always the best way to soothe myself during troubled times.

I do not like mob scenes, but individually or in small groups I was always approachable and especially glad to speak with other women of any age. Even today, if the occasional woman approaches me in a restaurant or shop and asks if I am Kim Vui, I will pause and be responsive. I really would rather not be recognized, but my personal desire for privacy should never excuse disrespecting another person who only wants to offer a friendly hello.

What do I think of postwar Viet Nam? Well, I generally agree with a young student from Hanoi, temporarily in America for graduate work, who expressed the opinion that there are three generations of the communist party leadership. The first, the Ho Chi Minh (not his birth name, but the name by which he became best known) generation, would do everything, justify anything, no matter how cruel, to achieve the goal of expelling the French colo-nial power. The second generation, the Le Duan group, would do everything, justify anything, no matter how cruel, to achieve the goal of defeating the southern separatist Republic of Viet Nam and discouraging American intervention.

The current generation of leadership will do everything, justify anything, no matter how cruel, to maintain themselves in power, and all for their own benefit. So, these days the two fundamental issues for Vietnamese are (1) how to cope with the powerful north-ern neighbor that aims to treat Viet Nam as a minor vassal and

(2) whether the Communist Party will ever allow alternative points of view, with citizens having real power to change policies and remove government officeholders.

My preoccupation and heartfelt concern are now more for America. The choices made, the sacrifices required in Viet Nam, will affect Vietnamese. But the choices and decisions made in the United States of America will impact every other country. Many nations envy, or even claim to hate, America, but still . . . they do want to have a working relationship with our country. We need to acknowledge that fact, develop intelligent policies, and be sure that when our word is given, we are making a sacred promise.

Whether by birth or immigration, it is both a privilege and a responsibility to be an American citizen. There is no other country like this one, founded on the premise that everyone is equal. Equality is protected by law but ultimately must be guaranteed by all of us. We are responsible for defending that principle. The way to do that is by joining with fellow citizens in civil political discourse and participating in every election.

There are, admittedly, stains on our history: treatment of Native Americans whereby treaties were made and quickly discarded; slavery and segregation with follow-on voter suppression; and detention with forced relocation of Japanese American citizens in 1942. But there are also truly glorious American achievements. Americans learn from adversity. Americans correct mistakes. Today we are multi-origin, multi-faith, and, albeit with some friction, more accepting of the need to stay politically and socially involved. I do not mean to lecture my American brothers and sisters; I simply hope you will appreciate that this child of Viet Nam understands.

I am proud that we of Vietnamese origin play a part in the evolving story of America, and it should be remembered that elected American leaders deliberately chose to make this possible. Beginning with Governor Bordallo in Guam, then President Ford, and later including President Jimmy Carter, those Americans, and

At home and reflecting upon a life of trial, tribulation, and finally . . . happiness.

others, understood the moral dimension of their choice to accept Vietnamese, increase the number allowed refuge, and provide a path for citizenship. Even when some suggested expedient alternatives, those men acted from their consciences and hearts. Although Governor Bordallo some fifteen years later committed suicide after a federal court convicted him of corruption during his second term of office, that does not diminish the principled decision he made for refugees in 1975. Today, Vietnamese Americans serve in our military at all grades including general officer. We are successful in business. We have a high rate of participation in every level of elections. We are Americans.

My own story is not finished because, to speak again of odds and ends, I was in fact shopping at a fabric store with an acquaintance when my cell phone rang. I usually do not pick up if the incoming number is unknown to me. That day, checking the screen for caller ID, I saw that it was Quoc Bao, a good friend who frequently performs as master of ceremony for nostalgic entertainment variety shows.

He told me that he was contacted by Tam Minh, daughter of a well-known former Republic of Viet Nam army officer and elected member of the southern national assembly, and that Tam Minh had asked him to be intermediary for enquiring whether I would accept a phone call from someone who wished to make an apology. She had promised Quoc Bao to relay my reply, whatever that might be. I thought this entirely strange and asked whether he was joking; if he were really serious, I should be given the name of the person supposedly in need of forgiveness.

"I am serious in this matter, as she is also," he replied, "and the person who hopes to speak with you is Frank Scotton."

My legs lost function, became non-supportive; I sagged upon a soft pile of several bolts of material not yet racked. Only that buffering cushion prevented me from sliding to the floor. My companion feared I had suffered a sudden stroke, and so I had . . . but not the medically defined sort that she supposed. The store employees were concerned, but I waved them off and weakly managed to gasp, not in my normal soft voice but very scratchily into my phone, a temporization.

"Tell them to give me a day," I murmured. I found it hard to believe that the green-eyed specter was still alive. If asked about him by anyone, I would have guessed that he had already died in some faraway land.

A day passed and then, on the very next, after a few rings, I opened my phone to see a strange caller ID number; I heard the voice that I had thought never to hear again. He may have been nervous—at least so he told me later—but he seemed to rather calmly explain that whenever recalling friends met and years spent in Viet Nam, he was deeply aware of, and regretful for, having treated me poorly. He asked whether he might see me and apologize in person as he had wanted to do for some fifty years. I responded, not really coolly but definitely not warmly either, simply with sincerity, that so many years had passed with our being on roads far apart that I now believed forgiveness unnecessary. But, if truly wished by him, he should know that I also understood the power of memory, and thus believed that his feeling of regret, after fifty years, was genuine. He asked again whether he might visit California to make his apology in person. I replied that a visit someday would be a welcome reminder, for both of us, of shared memories.

We spoke a few more times by telephone. He described having divorced his wife of more than forty years. It could not be a walk-away situation, because he had to ensure that she would have continuing health-care coverage and a fair portion of his retirement income. A few months passed, with frequent phone calls, and then finally he arrived at the Santa Ana airport.

We embraced, a warm hug between two old friends. At least, that is what I told myself. So, I could not understand the sudden dizzy feeling that came over me and the weakening in the knees. Even he, usually so assured, seemed almost awkward. Walking toward the parking garage, I was suddenly disoriented. I could not remember how to find the airport exit. I felt lost, unable to navigate homeward, and so called a friend on my cell phone to ask the best way from the airport to the 405 freeway.

For a million dollars, even more, I could not tell you what we spoke of on that drive to Garden Grove. I did ask whether Frank would like to stay in a hotel or take a room in my house, dreading the answer, whichever it might be. He responded that he would be honored, and grateful, to accept an invitation to stay in my home. After we arrived, I showed him the room toward the front of the house, already arranged . . . just in case.

I had two old Italian greyhounds, pests, but good company. They were surprised by having a strange visitor and, curious, followed Frank around as though he were bearing dog treats. While he took a shower, they clustered at his bedroom door, sniffing, indicating a canine assumption that he was there to visit with them rather than me. We went to a popular Vietnamese restaurant, Brodard, for a light meal. After returning home I asked Frank whether he would like to see the remainder of the house. A natural question, but I had not anticipated what next transpired.

My bedroom to the rear of the house looks outward to the garden where I spent hours cultivating tropical plants and trees. The view, with strung artificial lighting, is enchanting by night. But it was the bed that drew us by some gravitational magic. I spare myself confessional embarrassment by withholding intimate details. The reader will just have to rely on imagination.

We stayed in that bed a long time, talking, touching, and just holding onto each other while exchanging catch-up stories of where we had been, whom we knew, and what brought us back together. Well, one night was not enough for all of that, but it was a start. It is natural for a woman to wonder about her man's former wife. I was no different, and so I did ask what had happened.

Frank's explanation was that we had too soon parted and taken different directions. When the young woman he met in Taiwan became pregnant, he believed it would be shameful, and therefore impossible, to leave a child behind. Marriage was the solution. A few years later they had a daughter. From the beginning there was stress, but mutual concern for the children, and activities with them, was a sort of super glue. When their son and daughter were grown, living independently, the fundamental dissimilarities between the parents resurfaced. Both were unhappy.

I asked what would be next for him, really wondering what could be next for us. I knew, of course, that after half a century we two could not make a quick fix, but if any future at all for us might be possible, then what now?

True to his own history, the first step was to go away again. He planned to fly back to Florida, then load his car to drive cross country for California again. So typical of him: hit the road, just as he had from Saigon to Quang Tri, and years later, in Burma, from Rangoon to Mandalay and beyond.

Frank told me there were others from his past with whom he should reconnect to express either appreciation or regret. He could meet some of them while on the road. Some were in California, and he mentioned specifically Phan Manh Luong, then a Buddhist monk near San Diego; Tran Ngoc Chau, Stan Frileck, and Frank Snepp in Los Angeles; Bruce Landis in Long Beach; Jerry Dodson in San Francisco; and Douglas Ramsey not too far away in Nevada. Those are the ones I wrote down to remember. His personal list might have been longer. He concluded, "I am burdened by having disappointed you, more than I did anyone else."

A few months later he returned, almost hidden in a small SUV loaded to window level. At first Frank stayed in my home again, but then we both acknowledged that his being within my walls presumed too much too soon. We needed to find out whether our sense of the past, and thoughts of "maybe" a shared future, might fit together. Not so simple.

I helped him locate an apartment in Huntington Beach. It was a quick drive to the Mile Square Park tennis courts and not too far from where I lived. His daughter, Barbara, lived in Pasadena, and he could easily take the 405 and be with her an hour later. We spent time together almost every day, every evening, but very much without any strain of hasty commitment. Just as in Dalat long ago, we enjoyed night drives, through quiet neighborhoods, around the park, and along the Pacific Coast Highway. He held my hand, and I, his.

I asked why he had not sought me in 1970 or 1971 when he was back in Viet Nam and I was still there. He replied that when we had seen each other on a street in Saigon a year or so earlier, we both confessed to planning marriage to someone else.

"Had I looked for you in 1970 or 1971 it would have been an arrogant presumption imposed on you, disrespectful of you, and disrespectful of the woman I did marry. You might have wanted to shoot me."

Well, I certainly agreed, but I told him that it would have been with bow and arrow rather than with gun!

We were, as we had been long ago, comfortable together. Sometimes I stayed overnight with him in the apartment, and then more and more often. Eventually it seemed foolish to be going back and forth between two different addresses when we could, really wanted to, and therefore should, be together.

We were married in 2015 by a civil court in Orange County. Mindful of my mother's deep attachment to the Catholic Church, I hoped to find a way for the church to recognize us as a married couple. That was not easy because we had both been previously married, and Frank is a sort of Hoa Hao Buddhist. But we found an understanding priest, Timothy Nguyen, who, after meeting with us and documenting our history, obtained diocese approval for a church blessing of our civil marriage. Now we attend church every Sunday. Frank does not kneel, make the sign of the cross, or seek communion, but he is respectful. Meanwhile, he and a few friends play tennis every Wednesday morning with Timothy.

We are now two very different people, fifty-plus years after the evening when a young American introduced us in my Dalat coffee shop. Of course, one of our first long drives as husband and wife was to visit with Douglas Ramsey in Boulder City, Nevada. On that occasion we three took lunch in a nearby hotel restaurant, and after arranging ourselves by seating as we had in 1963 Dalat, a waitress snapped our photograph; the souvenir is as precious to me as the first one taken when we were young. We look different, but one can see strength in each face, the commitment to endure.

We visited Douglas more than once. On his last conscious day, while he could barely speak, I kissed his brow and murmured, "Thank you, and goodbye." We both had tears in our eyes. I was

After decades of separation, Frank and I drove to Nevada for a visit with Doug Ramsey, who had introduced us more than fifty years earlier before being captured and held prisoner for seven years.

thanking him for having introduced me to Frank and making my goodbye because we both understood that we would not meet again, not in this life.

I have read, but cannot remember from where, that "sometimes we worry about having made a wrong choice. Other times we fear loss of respect because of what people may think of us. We might be nervous about our future. The cause of all worry is a lack of confidence in one's own ability."

My personal code is to trust yourself. Have a sufficiently brave heart to exercise freedom of choice but be flexible enough to reconsider your decisions. Encourage others to be as strong as you want to be yourself. Be willing to forgive one who may have been in pain even while hurting you.

Now we two are in our garden, a small one, but made dense by trees (avocado, *long an*, papaya, lemon, orange, apple), flowering shrubs, and orchids. I sit here pondering my memories and thoughts shared with you. Frank is at the opposite side of the garden, barely visible because of the leafy interference. But I can make him out. He cannot escape my eye. He is cultivating with a narrow shovel, working around the roots of some plants that need consistent water.

He is not a good gardener. But he is right here, right now, and today that is better than good enough for me. Most of my life, for these past fifty years, I felt a deep hole within, but now it is filled by his constant presence.

Thinking again about the relativity of time, right now I wonder how best to live in a way so that a sense of time passing might slow rather than accelerate. How many more days will we have together? How much can I expect, hope for, when once again with the person loved more than fifty years earlier, that same person whose silhouette was permanently etched in my heart? These questions are especially sharp ones for me because of my having had a mini stroke a few years ago and spinal surgery even more recently. I do not know—no one could possibly know—when our time on earth will come to an end, but every shared day is precious.

Frank turns from scratching around in the dirt and smiles. I see him through the leaves . . . and then I am smiling, too.

This may be how many will remember me—following filming of *Chan Troi Tim* (The Purple Horizon)—as the "Sophia Loren of Viet Nam."

Index

CPSIA information can be obtained
at www.ICGtesting.com
Printed in the USA
LVHW030321050422
715324LV00004B/417